OCCASIO

IMF-Supported Programs in Indonesia, Korea, and Thailand
A Preliminary Assessment

Timothy Lane, Atish Ghosh, Javier Hamann, Steven Phillips,
Marianne Schulze-Ghattas, and Tsidi Tsikata

INTERNATIONAL MONETARY FUND
Washington DC
1999

Production: IMF Graphics Section
Typesetting: Alicia Etchebarne-Bourdin

Cataloging-in-Publication Data

IMF-supported programs in Indonesia, Korea, and Thailand : a preliminary assessment / by Timothy Lane . . . [et al.]. — [Washington DC : International Monetary Fund], 1999.

     p.   cm. — (Occasional paper, 0251-6365); no. 178
Includes bibliographical references.
ISBN 1-55775-783-6

  1. Indonesia—Economic policy. 2. Korea—Economic policy. 3. Thailand—Economic policy. 4. International Monetary Fund—Indonesia. 5. International Monetary Fund—Korea. 6. International Monetary Fund—Thailand. I. Lane, Timothy D. (Timothy David), 1955- II. Occasional paper (International Monetary Fund); no. 178.
HC447.I44 1999

Price: US$18.00
(US$15.00 to full-time faculty members and
students at universities and colleges)

Please send orders to:
International Monetary Fund, Publication Services
700 19th Street, N.W., Washington, D.C. 20431, U.S.A.
Tel.: (202) 623-7430   Telefax: (202) 623-7201
E-mail: publications@imf.org
Internet: http://www.imf.org

recycled paper

Contents

Figures

The following symbols have been used throughout this paper:

. . .   to indicate that data are not available;

—   to indicate that the figure is zero or less than half the final digit shown, or that the item does not exist;

–   between years or months (for example, 1994–95 or January–June) to indicate the years or months covered, including the beginning and ending years or months;

/   between years (for example, 1994/95) to indicate a crop or fiscal (financial) year.

"Billion" means a thousand million.

Minor discrepancies between constituent figures and totals are due to rounding.

The term "country," as used in this paper, does not in all cases refer to a territorial entity that is a state as understood by international law and practice; the term also covers some territorial entities that are not states, but for which statistical data are maintained and provided internationally on a separate and independent basis.

Preface

This paper is a preliminary review of the design of and early experience with IMF-supported programs in Indonesia, Korea, and Thailand during 1997–98. The review takes into account developments as of October 1998, and was the basis for a discussion of the programs by the IMF's Executive Board in December 1998. The review was prepared by a staff team from the Policy Development and Review Department under the direction of Jack Boorman, Director, and Thomas Leddy and Leslie Lipschitz, Deputy Directors. The staff team comprised Timothy Lane (Chief of the Policy Review Division), Atish Ghosh, Javier Hamann, Steven Phillips, Marianne Schulze-Ghattas, and Tsidi Tsikata.

The authors are grateful to numerous colleagues in the IMF as well as in the World Bank and the Asian Development Bank for detailed comments on drafts of the paper. Special thanks are due to those involved in work on the programs who provided data as well as their insights into the programs. Steven Symansky and other staff of the Fiscal Affairs Department provided the fiscal data that are the basis of the analysis in Section VII. The authors also wish to thank Kirsten Fitchett, Patricia Gillett-Lorusso, and Sibabrata Das for research assistance, and Olivia Carolin, Fernanda Gusmao, and Brian Gallo for secretarial support. Esha Ray of the External Relations Department edited the paper and coordinated production.

The opinions expressed in the paper are those of the IMF staff and do not necessarily reflect the views of national authorities or IMF Executive Directors.

I Overview

Timothy Lane and Marianne Schulze-Ghattas

The crisis that erupted in Asia's financial markets in 1997 has had dramatic effects on the countries involved: it precipitated deep recessions in these "tiger economies," resulting in a sharp drop of living standards together with rising unemployment and social dislocation. Moreover, the turbulence in financial markets has spread to other regions, and this, together with the sharp recession in Asia, constitutes an appreciable drag on world economic growth and has at times threatened to create an even wider crisis.

The Asian crisis differs from previous crises in key respects, and it may indicate fault lines in an increasingly integrated global economic and financial system. Unlike the typical case in which the IMF's assistance is requested, these crises did not result mainly from the monetization of fiscal imbalances and only in Thailand were there substantial external current account imbalances. Instead, they were rooted mainly in financial sector fragilities, stemming in part from weaknesses in governance in the corporate, financial, and government sectors, which made these economies increasingly vulnerable to changes in market sentiment, a deteriorating external situation, and contagion.

These distinctive features of the crisis needed to be taken into account in designing the policy responses in the context of IMF-supported programs. Macroeconomic policy adjustment was an essential element of the programs: monetary policy was aimed mainly at preventing a spiral of depreciation and inflation from emerging, while fiscal policy was initially intended mainly to provide some modest support for external adjustment and make room for the noninflationary financing of the carrying costs of the needed bank restructuring. But more than in previous IMF-supported programs, structural reforms, particularly in the financial sector and related areas, assumed a central role. These reforms were intended to address the root causes of the crisis, with a view to restoring market confidence and creating conditions for a sustainable resumption of growth. The strategy chosen, given the nature and scale of the crisis, entailed an unprecedented commitment of financial resources to break a self-reinforcing cycle of capital outflows, exchange rate depreciation, and financial sector weaknesses.

The IMF's support was organized under the Emergency Financing Mechanism. This mechanism, with a shortened period of negotiation, review, and approval by the IMF's Executive Board, permitted the programs to be put in place very quickly in response to immediate and overwhelming market pressures. At the same time, it forced exceptionally quick analysis by IMF staff and negotiations with country authorities. At times, decisions had to be based on more than usually incomplete information.

Economic events during the crisis have been dramatic and have defied expectations. As capital flows reversed, currencies depreciated precipitously. While the inflationary consequences of the depreciations in Korea and Thailand were reasonably well contained, in Indonesia inflation rose sharply. Growth plummeted in all three countries (as well as in other countries in the region), and external current accounts underwent abrupt swings. In several respects these outturns were much worse than expected: in particular, in all three countries there were sharp revisions to projections for growth and exchange rates, which necessitated significant changes in program targets. The revisions took into account new information about the magnitude of capital outflows, the deteriorating external environment more generally, and the worsening financial circumstances of domestic banks and corporations—as all of these developments exercised a self-aggravating influence over domestic demand and production. Some important economic vulnerabilities—notably the foreign exchange exposure of the financial and corporate sectors—became fully evident only as economies came under stress.

At this time, there remain risks to all the programs, with regard to both developments within the countries themselves and the external environment. The recession has continued to deepen in these countries as the balance sheet effects of the crisis work themselves out, and the success of reforms in tackling structural weaknesses and reestablishing growth on a sustainable basis is still not assured. Global economic developments, including the weak-

Box 1.1. Thailand: Crisis and Adjustment

Pressures on the baht, which had been evident already in late 1996, built up in the first half of 1997 against the background of an unsustainable current account deficit, significant appreciation of the real effective exchange rate, rising foreign debt (in particular, short term) a deteriorating fiscal balance, and increasing difficulties in the financial sector. Reserve money growth accelerated sharply as the Bank of Thailand provided liquidity support for ailing financial institutions. The policy response to the pressures in the exchange market focused on spot and forward intervention, introduction of controls on some capital account transactions, and limited measures to halt the weakening of the fiscal situation.

The exchange rate was floated on July 2, 1997, following mounting speculative attacks and concerns about the reserve position. The accompanying policy package was inadequate and failed to bolster market confidence. The baht depreciated by 20 percent against the U.S. dollar during July, while short-term interest rates were allowed to decline sharply after a temporary increase.

On August 20, 1997, the IMF's Executive Board approved a three-year Stand-By Arrangement with Thailand, amounting to $4 billion (505 percent of quota). Additional financing was pledged by the World Bank and the Asian Development Bank ($2.7 billion), which also provided extensive technical assistance. Financial support by Japan and other interested countries ($10 billion) was pledged at a meeting in August, hosted by Japan. Bilateral financing has been disbursed in parallel with the purchases from the IMF. The underlying adjustment program was aimed at restoring confidence, bringing about an orderly reduction in the current account deficit, reconstituting foreign exchange reserves, and limiting the rise in inflation to the one-off effects of the depreciation. Growth was expected to decelerate sharply, but to remain positive. Key elements of the policy package included measures to restructure the financial sector (including closure of insolvent financial institutions); fiscal adjustment measures equivalent to some 3 percent of GDP to bring the fiscal balance back into surplus and contribute to shrinking the current account deficit; and control of domestic credit, with indicative ranges for interest rates. The baht continued to float and foreign exchange market intervention was to be limited to smoothing. Upon approval of the program, Thailand drew $1.2 billion from the IMF and received a further $4 billion from bilateral and multilateral sources.

In the subsequent months, the baht continued to depreciate as rollover of short-term debt declined and the crisis in Asia spread. While macroeconomic policies were on track and nominal interest rates were raised (albeit subject to considerable short-term fluctuations), market confidence was adversely affected by delays in the implementation of financial sector reforms, political uncertainty, and initial difficulties in communicating key aspects of the program. By the time of the review under the emergency financing procedures (October 17, 1997), there were also signs that the slowdown of economic activity would be more pronounced than anticipated. A new government took office in mid-November 1997.

To help stabilize the exchange market situation, the program was strengthened at the first quarterly review (December 8, 1997). With weakening economic activity constraining revenues, additional fiscal measures were introduced to achieve the original fiscal target for 1997/98.[1] Reserve money and net domestic assets of the Bank of Thailand were to be kept below the original program limits, the indicative range for interest rates

---

[1]The fiscal year begins in October.

---

ness of the Japanese economy, turbulence in emerging markets in other regions, and the sharp decline in commodity prices, also pose risks to the stabilization process and could delay economic recovery. There are signs, however, that the recessions in these countries are bottoming out and financial market conditions are stabilizing.

This paper represents the first systematic review within the IMF of the policy response to the crisis, and possible lessons for future practice.[1] Given the fact that events are still unfolding and programs are still in the process of revision, it will necessarily be selective in the questions it addresses and provisional in the answers it provides. The study covers the period through October 1998. The paper also takes a narrow approach in the countries examined: it focuses primarily on events in Indonesia, Korea, and Thailand (Boxes 1.1–1.3), even though further useful lessons might be drawn by examining other countries in the region—notably Malaysia and the Philippines—in which many of the same forces were at work. Malaysia is excluded because it did not have an IMF-supported program, the Philippines (although it has had a program) because its recent history was quite different from the other crisis countries.

Section II briefly reviews the origins of the Asian financial crisis in financial sector fragilities—notably the large short-term foreign currency debt of domestic financial institutions and corporations, together with inflated domestic asset prices and deteriorating loan quality—that made these economies vulnerable to a deteriorating external situation and market contagion, particularly given the volatility of

---

[1]The World Bank has published a report, entitled *East Asia: The Road to Recovery* reviewing the crisis and charting the way ahead.

was raised, and a specific timetable for financial sector restructuring was announced.

After falling to an all-time low against the U.S. dollar in early January 1998, the baht began to strengthen in early February as improvements in the policy setting revived market confidence amid an upturn in regional markets more generally. Growth projections, however, were marked down further. Contracting domestic demand helped to keep inflation in check and contributed to a larger-than-expected adjustment in the current account.

In view of stabilizing exchange market conditions and the changed economic outlook, the program was revised significantly at the time of the second quarterly review (March 4, 1998). Under the revised program, monetary policy continued to focus on the exchange rate, with interest rates to be maintained high until evidence of a sustained stabilization emerged. Fiscal policy shifted to a more accommodating stance, allowing automatic stabilizers to take effect. In addition, the program included measures to strengthen the social safety net, and broadened the scope of structural reforms to strengthen the core banking system and promote corporate restructuring.

The third quarterly review (June 10, 1998) took place against the background of a marked strengthening of the baht during February–May 1998 (some 35 percent vis-à-vis the U.S. dollar from the low in January), and stronger-than-expected foreign exchange reserves, but a deepening recession. The revised program was on track, but with real GDP now projected to decline by 4–5 percent in 1998 and inflation subdued, further adjustments were made to allow for an increase in the fiscal deficit target for 1997/98 from 2 percent to 3 percent of GDP. Monetary policy continued to focus on maintaining the stability of the baht. While the cau-

tious reduction of interest rates since late March 1998 was viewed as consistent with exchange market developments, it was understood that interest rates would be raised again if necessary. Additional measures to strengthen the social safety net were planned, and the program for financial sector and corporate restructuring was further specified.

The exchange rate weakened somewhat during June–July 1998 amid growing concerns about the growth outlook, and renewed signs of strain in the financial sector. Fiscal and monetary policy had been tighter than programmed, activity was weaker than expected, and exports had failed to pick up. The large adjustment in the current account (projected to amount to over 10 percent of GDP in 1998) reflected a sharp compression of imports. Restructuring of financial institutions was complicated by growing difficulties in the corporate sector.

The fourth quarterly review (completed on September 11, 1998) focused on adapting the policy framework to support the recovery without sacrificing stabilization gains. With output now projected to decline by 6–8 percent in 1998, efforts were stepped up to utilize the scope for fiscal easing provided under the program. Foreign exchange market conditions were relatively stable (in spite of the Russian crisis), providing room for a further lowering of interest rates. The program for financial and corporate sector restructuring was broadened significantly, and the structural reform agenda in other areas (privatization, foreign ownership, and social safety net) was strengthened.

As of October 19, 1998, $12.2 billion of the total financing package for Thailand ($17.2 billion) had been disbursed, including $3 billion from the IMF and $9.2 billion from other multilateral (World Bank and Asian Development Bank) and bilateral sources.

short-term capital flows in international markets. The monetization of fiscal imbalances and evident exchange rate misalignments, prevalent in many countries that seek IMF support, played a lesser role, except in Thailand.

The basic strategy of the programs formulated to address the crisis are discussed in Section III. Macroeconomic policies were an essential element of these programs; and large official financing packages were assembled to help break a self-reinforcing cycle of capital outflows, exchange rate depreciation, and financial sector weakness. But more than in previous IMF-supported programs, structural reforms, particularly in the financial sector and related areas, took a central role. Indeed, it was structural reforms that were needed to address the root causes of the crisis, restore market confidence, and set the stage for a sustainable resumption of growth. The section also examines the decision to allow ex-

change rates to continue floating, arguing that there was no viable alternative since repegging would have required subordinating monetary policy exclusively to the defense of the currency and, given available reserves and financing, the rate that would be defensible against short-run market pressures would have been too depreciated to be appropriate for the medium term.

Section IV addresses issues related to program financing and market reactions. Financing needs were dominated by the huge potential volume of capital outflows. In each of the programs, very large official financing packages, together with sound economic policies, were intended to restore confidence and limit private capital outflows. However, the programs were not initially successful in restoring confidence, and private capital outflows far exceeded program projections. Restoring confidence quickly was intrinsically difficult given the state of their re-

Box 1.2. Indonesia: The Deepening Crisis

In July 1997, soon after the floating of the Thai baht, pressure on the rupiah intensified. Key macroeconomic indicators in Indonesia were stronger than in Thailand (the current account deficit had been modest, export growth had been reasonably well maintained, and the fiscal balance had remained in surplus), but Indonesia's short-term private sector external debt had been rising rapidly, and growing evidence of weaknesses in the financial sector raised doubts about the government's ability to defend the currency peg.

Following a widening of the intervention band on July 11, 1997, the rupiah was floated on August 14, 1997. The exchange rate depreciated sharply but recovered temporarily in response to a tightening of liquidity and measures to prevent a deterioration of the fiscal balance as economic activity began to slow. Exchange market pressures heightened again in late September as monetary conditions were eased in view of increasing strains in the financial sector. With the rupiah falling further against the U.S. dollar, by early October, the cumulative depreciation since early July (over 30 percent) became the largest in the region.

On November 5, 1997, the IMF's Executive Board approved a three-year Stand-By Arrangement with Indonesia equivalent to $10 billion (490 percent of quota). Additional financing commitments included $8 billion from the World Bank and the Asian Development Bank, which also provided extensive technical assistance, and pledges from interested countries amounting to some $18 billion as a second line of defense. The key objectives of the underlying adjustment program were to restore market confidence, bring about an orderly adjustment in the current account, limit the unavoidable decline in output growth, and contain the inflationary impact of exchange rate depreciation. The main elements of the policy package included tight monetary policy, combined, if necessary, with exchange market intervention to stabilize the rupiah; measures to strengthen the underlying fiscal position to facilitate current account adjustment; a plan to strengthen the financial sector (including closure of nonviable institutions); and an initial set of structural reforms to enhance efficiency and transparency in the corporate sector. Upon approval of the program, Indonesia drew $3 billion from the IMF.

The initial response to the program was positive, and the rupiah strengthened briefly. A tightening of liquidity and concerted exchange market intervention temporarily boosted market confidence and the exchange rate.

Difficulties soon reemerged, however, and the exchange rate fell precipitously during December 1997–January 1998. While the current account improved, capital outflows increased and reserves declined sharply. Key factors contributing to the deterioration included stop-and-go monetary policy, vacillating between support for the exchange rate and strong liquidity expansion in the face of financial sector strain and runs on deposits; uneven implementation of important structural measures, signaling lack of commitment to the program; and political uncertainty in light of concerns about the president's health and the forthcoming presidential election. The budget for 1998/99[1] announced on January 6, 1998 reinforced market concerns about the government's commitment to the program.

A strengthened program was announced on January 15, 1998 to reverse the decline of the rupiah, but market reaction was skeptical. The program included a commitment to tight monetary policy and a comprehensive package of structural reforms prepared in cooperation with the World Bank; a comprehensive bank-restructuring plan followed soon after (although in hindsight the program did not move quickly enough to address the problems of corporate debt). Implementation of the structural reform agenda, however, continued to lag, and the macroeconomic program quickly ran off track, with base money growing rapidly, fueled by Bank Indonesia's liquidity support for financial institutions. Program implementation was sidetracked by discussions about the introduction of a currency board and preparations for the March presidential election. The economic downturn deepened, while inflation accelerated sharply. In view of the political situation, the first quarterly review was delayed until April 1998.

Following the formation of a new government after the reelection of the president, the first review was completed on May 4, 1998 on the basis of a modified program. With the economy now on the verge of a vicious circle of currency depreciation and hyperinflation, the main objectives of the revised program were to stabilize the exchange rate at a more realistic level and to reduce inflation. In addition, the program sought to limit the decline in output, eventually restore growth, and protect the

---

[1]The fiscal year begins in April.

---

serves, the volatility of market sentiment, and the array of structural problems that had to be dealt with. Several factors contributed to weak confidence, including hesitant program implementation, political uncertainties and other factors casting doubt on the authorities' commitment to the programs, the revelation of market-sensitive information, problems with the coverage of government guarantees, and uncertainties surrounding the financing packages. The experience underscores the importance of further work on the architecture of the international financial system, including more effective ways of involving the private sector in the event of a crisis.

Section V discusses the macroeconomic developments associated with the crisis, notably the deep recessions related to massive current account adjustments. Domestic demand declined sharply, reflecting precipitous drops in fixed investment and, poor from the worst effects of the crisis. The policy package included a tightening of monetary policy, with sharply higher interest rates and strict control over the central bank's net domestic assets; an adjusted fiscal framework that took into account the less favorable outlook for growth and allowed for the cost of bank restructuring as well as expenditures to cushion the impact of the crisis on the poor; a strengthened plan for the restructuring of the banking system; and an expanded set of far-reaching structural reforms (including privatization and the dismantling of monopolies and price controls) to improve efficiency, transparency, and governance in the corporate sector. In addition, talks on agreements with private creditors regarding the restructuring of corporate sector obligations and the rollover of short-term bank debt were under way. To enhance program monitoring, a temporary move to monthly reviews was agreed.

The program was cast off track by severe civil unrest, which led to the resignation of President Suharto on May 21, 1998. Production, exports, and domestic supply channels were disrupted, banking activities were paralyzed, unemployment was rising, and food prices were soaring. The rupiah nose-dived and hit an all-time low of 16,650 against the U.S. dollar in mid-June 1998, with a cumulative depreciation of 85 percent since June 1997.

An agreement with a steering committee of private creditors was reached on June 4, 1998. The agreement covered the restructuring of interbank debt falling due before end-March 1999, a trade facility to help restore normal trade financing, and a framework for the voluntary restructuring of corporate debt involving a government exchange guarantee scheme (INDRA scheme).

By the time of the second review (July 15, 1998) the program had to contend with major dislocations. Output was now expected to decline by 10–15 percent in 1998/99, and inflation was projected to average 60 percent. Restoration of the distribution system and a strengthening of the social safety net became key immediate priorities. Monetary policy remained focused on inflation and the exchange rate, while the fiscal deficit target was adjusted significantly in view of the sharp contraction of output and special expenditure requirements. Bank-restructuring plans were strengthened to deal with the deteriorating conditions in the financial system, and further steps were taken to facilitate corporate debt restructuring. Access under the Stand-By Arrangement was increased by the equivalent of $1 billion.

In view of the deep-seated nature of Indonesia's structural and balance of payments problems, the IMF's Executive Board on August 25, 1998 approved the authorities' request to replace the Stand-By Arrangement by an Extended Arrangement with the same access ($6.3 billion, or 312 percent of quota, for the remaining 26 months)[2] and phasing as envisaged under the Stand-By Arrangement. Additional financing sources included $2 billion from the World Bank and the Asian Development Bank, close to $1 billion from bilateral sources, and a prospective rescheduling of external debt to official creditors. Macroeconomic policies were broadly on track and commitments concerning structural policies were strengthened in several areas, notably in the subsidy and distribution system and financial and corporate sector restructuring. The program has been monitored closely, with the second monthly review completed on October 30, 1998.

On September 23, 1998, an agreement was reached on the rescheduling or refinancing of Indonesia's bilateral external debt to official creditors. The agreement covers principal payments on official debt (excluding public enterprises) and export credit for the period August 6, 1998 to March 31, 2000 ($4.1 billion in total).

As of October 1998 market sentiment had improved and the rupiah had appreciated significantly, providing room for lowering interest rates. Fiscal targets were eased further in light of the deteriorating economic outlook. The output decline in 1998 is expected to be contained at 15 percent and year-end inflation at 80 percent, with a marked deceleration in the last months of 1998. The current account is expected to register a surplus of some 4 percent of GDP. The structural reform agenda has been broadened further, but implementation has been somewhat uneven, particularly in the area of corporate restructuring.

At the end of September 1998, $9.5 billion of the augmented financing package for Indonesia ($42 billion)[3] had been disbursed (most of which—almost $5.7 billion—was disbursed since end-April 1998), including $6.8 billion from the IMF, $1.3 billion from the World Bank and the Asian Development Bank, and $1.4 billion from bilateral sources.

---

[2]Including augmentation of the IMF Stand-By Arrangement.
[3]Including debt rescheduling and new funds to be provided in lieu of rescheduling.

to a lesser extent, in private consumption, while external demand did not provide as much support for economic activity as had been hoped. The IMF, like most observers, misread the extent of the recession—in part because, as in all IMF-supported programs, macroeconomic projections were predicated on the programs' proceeding as planned.

Section VI discusses monetary policy, which sought to balance the goal of preventing a spiral of exchange rate depreciation and inflation against concerns that excessive monetary tightening could severely weaken economic activity. The policy adopted was to lean against the wind in the foreign exchange market rather than pursuing any particular exchange rate target. In Korea and Thailand, policies were tightened as envisaged in the monetary program; by the summer of 1998, interest rates had returned to precrisis levels, and over half of the sharp

Box 1.3. Korea: Crisis and Adjustment

Korea initially appeared relatively little affected by the crisis in the region, with the exchange rate remaining broadly stable through October 1997. However, with a high level of short-term debt and only moderate international reserves, the economy was vulnerable to a shift in market sentiment. While macroeconomic fundamentals were relatively favorable, concerns about the soundness of financial institutions and *chaebol* had increased significantly in the wake of several large corporate bankruptcies earlier in the year. As Korean banks began to face difficulties rolling over their short-term foreign liabilities, the Bank of Korea shifted foreign exchange reserves to the banks' offshore branches and the government announced a guarantee of foreign borrowing by Korean banks.

External financing conditions deteriorated significantly in late October 1997 and the won fell sharply while usable foreign exchange reserves declined rapidly. Monetary policy was tightened briefly, but was relaxed again in light of concerns about the impact of higher interest rates on the highly leveraged corporate sector. By early December 1997, the won had depreciated by over 20 percent against the U.S. dollar and usable foreign exchange reserves had declined to $6 billion (from $22.5 billion at the end of October 1997).

On December 4, 1997, the IMF's Executive Board approved a three-year Stand-By Arrangement with Korea, amounting to $21 billion (1,939 percent of quota). Financing amounting to $14 billion had been committed by the World Bank and the Asian Development Bank, which also provided extensive technical assistance. In addition, interested countries had pledged $22 billion as a second line of defense for a total package of $58.4 billion. To establish conditions for an early return of market confidence, the underlying program aimed to bring about an orderly reduction in the current account deficit, build up foreign exchange reserves, and contain inflation through a tightening of monetary policy and some fiscal measures. In addition, the program included a range of structural reforms in the financial and corporate sectors to address the root causes of the

crisis. Upon approval of the program, Korea drew $5.5 billion from the IMF.

The positive impact of the announcement of the program on exchange and stock markets was small and short-lived. In the two weeks to the first biweekly review, the won dropped sharply. Confidence was undermined by doubts about the commitment to the program as the leading candidates for the December 18, 1997 presidential election hesitated to endorse it publicly. Moreover, with new information becoming available about the state of financial institutions, the level of usable reserves, and short-term obligations falling due, markets became concerned about a widening financing gap.

With rollover of short-term debt down sharply, usable international reserves nearly exhausted, and the won in free fall, a temporary agreement was reached with private bank creditors on December 24, 1997 to maintain exposure, and discussions on voluntary rescheduling of short-term debt were initiated. Korea requested a rephasing of purchases under the Stand-By Arrangement on December 30, 1997, to permit an advancement of drawings. At the same time, the structural reform agenda of the program was strengthened to accelerate financial sector restructuring and facilitate capital inflows into the domestic stock and bond market. Interest rates had been raised significantly, and conditions for the provision of foreign currency liquidity support to banks had been tightened.

By the time of the second biweekly review on January 8, 1998, signs of stabilization emerged. Rollover rates increased significantly after the agreement with the banks; usable international reserves stabilized, and the won appreciated moderately against the U.S. dollar. The current account had moved into surplus, but owing to the large depreciation of the exchange rate, inflation was now expected to exceed original program projections. In addition, there were growing concerns about the deceleration of economic activity.

On January 28, 1998, Korea reached an agreement in principle with private bank creditors on a voluntary rescheduling of short-term debt. The agreement covered

initial exchange rate depreciation had been reversed. In Indonesia, in contrast, monetary developments went seriously off track because of political turbulence and extreme financial system weaknesses; macroeconomic turmoil, spiraling inflation, rising risk premiums, continued capital flight, and a dramatic collapse of economic activity followed, with the situation stabilizing only in the latter months of 1998. The section assesses the stance of monetary policy in the three countries and concludes that in Indonesia, monetary policy was not tight—on the contrary, the authorities lost control of money and credit, and nominal interest rates and the exchange rate were driven by market risk premiums while un-

derlying real interest rates remained negative. A more difficult question is whether the Thai and Korean programs' successful stabilization caused monetary conditions to become too tight, contributing excessively to the contraction in economic activity; a variety of monetary indicators examined in the section suggest that monetary tightening in these countries was not extreme (in degree or duration) in relation to other crises elsewhere. At the same time, reports of disruptions in credit allocation, possibly reflecting heightened perceptions of risk, while common to most crisis situations, are of concern; the section reviews some evidence on the nature of these disruptions.

interbank deposits and short-term loans maturing during 1998, equivalent to some $22 billion.

The first quarterly review of the Stand-By Arrangement (February 17, 1998) took place against the background of an improving exchange market situation and growing signs of a pronounced decline in economic activity. The agreement with bank creditors had helped to improve financing conditions, usable reserves had increased, and the won had appreciated by nearly 20 percent from the low in late December 1997. With domestic demand contracting, the revised program was based on lower (but still marginally positive) growth projections. The fiscal target for 1998 was lowered from a surplus of 0.2 percent of GDP in the original program (including bank-restructuring costs) to a deficit of 0.8 percent of GDP. Monetary policy was expected to remain tight as long as the exchange market situation continued to be fragile. While a number of steps had already been taken to implement the program's comprehensive structural reform agenda, commitments in several areas, notably financial sector restructuring and capital account and trade liberalization, were further specified. In addition, based on a tripartite accord between business, labor, and the government, the agenda was broadened to include measures to strengthen the social safety net, increase labor market flexibility, promote corporate restructuring, and enhance corporate governance. A new government took office in late February 1998.

The program remained on track and market confidence in the new government's commitment strengthened, but growth projections were marked down further during the second quarterly review (completed on May 29, 1998). Korea had successfully launched a global sovereign bond issue, significant capital inflows into the domestic stock and bond market had been registered, and usable reserves exceeded $30 billion. The sharp decline in economic activity, however, was weighing heavily on corporations, necessitating an acceleration of structural reforms in the financial and corporate sectors. Interest rates had been lowered cautiously, but monetary policy continued to focus on maintaining exchange market stability. In view of the weaker outlook for growth, the fiscal target was lowered further to permit automatic stabilizers to take effect.

By July 1998, Korea had made substantial progress in overcoming its external crisis. Market sentiment weakened somewhat in June in view of growing concerns about the domestic recession and the impact of economic conditions in the region. The won remained broadly stable, however, and appreciated vis-à-vis the U.S. dollar in July, permitting a further easing of interest rates. Interest rates declined further to precrisis levels, and a supplementary budget was under preparation to support economic activity and strengthen the social safety net. Output was projected to decline by 4 percent in 1998, inflation had decelerated and was expected to average 9 percent during the year, and the current account surplus was expected to reach nearly $35 billion (over 10 percent of GDP).

The third quarterly review (August 28, 1998) focused on a further easing of macroeconomic policies to mitigate the severity of the recession, and a strengthening of the structural reform agenda. Output was projected to contract by 5 percent in 1998, inflation had decelerated further and was expected to average 8.5 percent during the year, and the current account surplus was still expected to reach nearly $35 billion (10 percent of GDP). Exchange market conditions permitting, interest rates were to be lowered further. The fiscal deficit target was raised to 4 percent of GDP and a supplementary budget was introduced to increase expenditures, including, in particular, for social programs. Structural reforms emphasized the rationalization and strengthening of the banking system as well as corporate restructuring, which was to be broadened significantly with support from the World Bank.

At the end of October 1998, $27.2 billion of the total financing package for Korea ($58.2 billion) had been disbursed, including $18.2 billion from the IMF and $9 billion from the World Bank and the Asian Development Bank.

Fiscal policies are examined in Section VII. The initial programs, predicated on the assumption that the slowdown in growth would be modest, planned some fiscal adjustment to offset a weakening of fiscal positions, support external adjustment without an excessive squeeze on the private sector's financing, and make room for the costs of bank restructuring and social safety nets. If these deficit targets had been implemented under the macroeconomic conditions that emerged, they would have implied an excessively contractionary policy. However, beginning early in 1998, as the recession deepened and current accounts shifted into large surpluses owing to sagging domestic demand and large currency deprecia-tions, fiscal policy became increasingly oriented toward supporting economic activity. Fiscal deficits were allowed to increase considerably in all three countries to accommodate part of the effects of the automatic stabilizers and the exchange rate depreciation on the fiscal positions. More recently, programs turned more expansionary, augmenting these automatic effects through discretionary measures. In Indonesia and Korea, however, it has proved difficult to adjust spending rapidly to use the leeway for fiscal stimulus allowed under the program ceilings.

Section VIII examines the strategy of structural reform in the programs, which were intended to address the structural weaknesses underlying the crisis and create the basis for a return to sustainable growth. The initial IMF-supported programs provided an overall framework of action for the next three years, including aspects to be dealt with—and spelled out in more detail—by the World Bank and the Asian Development Bank. The section first assesses the strategy of financial sector restructuring, which included two broad strands: handling the crisis and its aftermath and implementing reforms to minimize the likelihood of recurrence. Given the need for immediate action as well as the large number and variety of issues that had to be dealt with, the strategy for financial and corporate sector restructuring inevitably evolved with events and with deepening understanding of the problems. Some key lessons that emerge are a need to elaborate the IMF's policies in the area of financial crisis management (including the coverage of government guarantees) as well as financial and corporate restructuring; the need to treat corporate restructuring as part and parcel of financial sector restructuring; and the need to give early priority to addressing deficiencies in the institutional and legal framework for financial and corporate sector restructuring. The section also discusses other aspects of structural reform, including measures to address deficiencies in governance and market discipline, as well as to advance trade and capital account liberalization. Social sector policies were regarded as an integral part of the programs: concerns about the impact of the crisis on the poorest and most vulnerable segments of society were expressed from the outset and became more pressing as the domestic recession deepened. The section notes that concerns that the programs were overloaded with structural measures, some of which might better have been delayed until later, cannot entirely be dismissed—and, indeed, as the programs evolved the focus on the key financial and corporate issues sharpened. At the same time, the urgency of the crisis and complementarities among different reforms called for many steps to be taken simultaneously. Such concerns may point to a need for further consideration of the appropriate pace and sequencing of reforms.

Section IX presents some concluding remarks.

References

Corsetti, Giancarlo, Paolo Pesenti, and Nouriel Roubini, 1998, "What Caused the Asian Currency and Financial Crisis?" (unpublished; New York: New York University).

Goldstein, Morris, 1998, *The Asian Financial Crisis: Causes, Cures, and Systemic Implications* (Washington: Institute for International Economics).

International Monetary Fund, 1997, *World Economic Outlook, December 1997: A Survey by the Staff of the International Monetary Fund,* World Economic and Financial Surveys (Washington).

World Bank, 1998, *East Asia: The Road to Recovery* (Washington).

II Background to the Crisis

Javier Hamann

In many respects, the Asian crisis differed from previous financial crises that created a need for the IMF's assistance. It was rooted primarily in financial system vulnerabilities and other structural weaknesses, and it occurred in the context of unprecedentedly rapid moves toward financial market globalization. Conventional fiscal imbalances were relatively small; and only in Thailand were significant real exchange rate misalignments evident.

Despite several differences in specific aspects of the crisis in Indonesia, Korea, and Thailand, some broad similarities are evident across the three countries. In all three countries, weaknesses in financial systems, stemming from inadequate regulation and supervision and (to varying degrees) a tradition of government guarantees and a heavy governmental role in credit allocation—and weaknesses in governance at a more general and fundamental level—had been evident in the misallocation of credit and inflated asset prices. Another critical fragility that all three countries shared was associated with large unhedged private short-term foreign currency debt in a setting where corporations were highly geared; in Korea and Thailand, this debt was mainly intermediated through the banking system, while in Indonesia the corporations had heavier direct exposures to such debt. Economic and financial data that were inadequate for making informed decisions contributed to these imbalances, as did inadequate risks assessment and low interest rates in creditor countries. The limited degree of exchange rate variability prior to the crisis encouraged the large-scale, unhedged foreign currency borrowing, also making currencies vulnerable to speculative attacks.

Short-term foreign-currency-denominated debt created two kinds of vulnerabilities in these economies. First, fears that spark liquidity attacks can be self-fulfilling, analogous to the possibility of bank runs in the absence of deposit insurance.[1] If other creditors are pulling their money out, each individual creditor has an incentive to join the queue, and the result is that even a debtor that had been fully solvent before the attack could be plunged into insolvency.[2] A second vulnerability is associated with the exchange rate exposures such debt entails; to varying degrees in the three countries, exchange risk was either borne by financial institutions, passed on to corporations as the funds were on-lent (thereby converting exchange risk into credit risk, from the financial institutions' standpoint), or borne directly by corporations that engaged in foreign borrowing. These elements are further complicated by the interaction of exchange rate and credit risks: if currency depreciation, possibly resulting from a liquidity attack, leads to widespread insolvency, this creates additional counterparty risk that adds momentum to the exit of capital. Any decline in market confidence can thus become both self-sustaining and contagious across countries.

In this setting, even a moderate deterioration in macroeconomic conditions could have a disproportionate effect. In 1996, following years of rapid growth, all three countries experienced a deceleration of export growth coupled with a negative terms-of-trade shock, which put pressure on external balances and domestic economic activity. As growth slowed, the quality of asset portfolios deteriorated further and the underlying weaknesses in the financial sector became increasingly evident, raising concerns among foreign investors about the creditworthiness of financial institutions. In addition, financial sector fragilities heightened the cost of using interest rates to defend prevailing exchange rate regimes, raising doubts about the authorities' willingness to defend their currencies should a speculative attack occur.

Financial tensions had been evident in all three countries for some time before the crisis. They were particularly severe in Thailand, where macroeco-

---

[1]This risk does not depend on the unhedged nature of the borrowing, since in general a currency hedge does not protect against liquidity and credit risks.

[2]The case of a self-sustaining bank run, whereby a previously solvent bank that undergoes a bank run may have to liquidate assets on unfavorable terms and thereby become insolvent, has been analyzed by Diamond and Dybvig (1983). This pattern, where self-fulfilling expectations lead to a change in fundamentals, is the essence of so-called second generation models of speculative attacks; for a review of these models, see for instance Obstfeld (1996). Radelet and Sachs (1998) focus on the role of this kind of self-justifying behavior in the Asian crisis.

nomic imbalances, reflected in a large current account deficit and an overvalued real exchange rate, were more pronounced than in the other two countries. Following months of financial turbulence and speculative activities in the foreign exchange market, Thailand was forced to float the baht on July 2, 1997 in the face of serious difficulties in rolling over short-term debt and a depletion of net foreign exchange reserves. Strong downward pressures on the currency drove the authorities to request an exceptionally large Stand-By Arrangement with the IMF. In the ensuing months, the currency continued to depreciate, accompanied by mounting liquidity and insolvency problems in both financial and nonfinancial institutions. The financial vulnerabilities made it easy for the crisis to spread throughout the region, notably to Indonesia and Korea, which also requested IMF arrangements with access far above the usual limits; these arrangements were approved by the IMF's Executive Board in November (Indonesia) and early December (Korea).[3]

This background to the crisis is discussed below, drawing on more detailed treatments elsewhere,[4] to set the stage for presenting the strategy of the programs later in the paper.

Financial Vulnerabilities

Stock imbalances at various levels were at the core of financial sector fragilities in the crisis countries. They were rooted in deep-seated structural weaknesses, including a long history of promoting domestic investment through policy loans and guarantees for corporate debtors, which obviated the need for thorough risk assessment; implicit guarantees on banks' liabilities, which did not encourage close monitoring of financial institutions by depositors and other creditors;[5] and lax regulatory frameworks, which failed to set and enforce standards for sound banking operations. Another factor was connected lending: that is, the tight connections between banks and borrowing customers (for example, the ownership of weakly reg-

ulated banks by nonfinancial corporations in Indonesia). This environment created incentives for lenders to take high risks and encouraged excessive borrowing to finance risky and often doubtful investment projects.[6] As a result, banks' balance sheets exhibited substantial amounts of nonperforming loans,[7] increasing exposures to the property sector,[8] large holdings of corporate stocks (mainly in Korea), and low capital-asset ratios. Many insolvent financial institutions were permitted to continue operations. In Korea and Thailand, large corporations were highly leveraged, aided, among other things, by a complex system of debt guarantees within *chaebol* (Korea) and a relatively generous tax treatment of corporate debt compared to equity (Thailand).[9]

These imbalances were compounded and at the same time obscured by large capital inflows which, together with high domestic savings, helped fuel strong investment and growth. These capital flows also reflected conditions in the global financial system, including low interest rates and weaknesses in risk management in industrial countries. In 1990–96, net capital inflows averaged an annual 10 percent of GDP in Thailand, 3½ percent in Indonesia, and 2½ percent in Korea. Financial institutions played an important role in intermediating these inflows (especially in Korea and Thailand) or by providing guarantees on direct foreign borrowing by corporations. While, on the whole, the IMF and the authorities were aware of the magnitude of these inflows, and some concern was expressed, this concern was tempered by the perception that the inflows were attributable mainly to favorable investment prospects associated with a stable macroeconomic environment and high growth. In hindsight, however, it appears that the inflows were to a considerable extent financing asset price inflation and an accumulation of poor-quality loans in the portfolios of banks and other financial intermediaries.

---

[3]The evolution of exchange rates through the crisis is shown in Figure 6.1 (Section VI). For a detailed chronology of the crisis, see International Monetary Fund (1997).

[4]For instance, International Monetary Fund (1997); Charles Adams and others (1998); and various academic studies. Three recent outside studies of the crisis are Corsetti, Pesenti, and Roubini (1998); Goldstein (1998); and Radelet and Sachs (1998).

[5]Despite the absence of formal deposit insurance, holders of deposits in the domestic financial institutions in these countries may well have operated under the assumption that the government guaranteed those deposits and thus felt no need to keep close track of these institutions' soundness. While this is a feature of most countries' banking systems, it creates a need for effective supervision to ensure that institutions do not take excessive risks, but such supervision was lacking.

[6]This explanation of the crisis is elaborated in Krugman (1998) and Dooley (1997).

[7]Official precrisis estimates of nonperforming loans generally underestimated their magnitude. For a comparison of official and unofficial estimates of nonperforming loans in Indonesia, Korea and Thailand, see Berg (forthcoming).

[8]By end-1997 the share of loans to the property sector in total loans was of the order of 30–40 percent in Thailand, 20–30 percent in Indonesia, and 15–25 percent in Korea. See Goldstein (1998), p. 8.

[9]In Korea and Thailand, for example, average ratios of corporate debt to equity were 395 percent and 450 percent, respectively. Such ratios elsewhere, including in Asia, tend to be much lower (for instance, in Germany, 144 percent; Malaysia, 160; Japan, 194; Sweden, 154; Taiwan, Province of China, 90; and the United States, 106). These high debt-equity ratios also reflected features of the tax system, including the absence of thin capitalization rules and comparatively low effective tax rates on interest income.

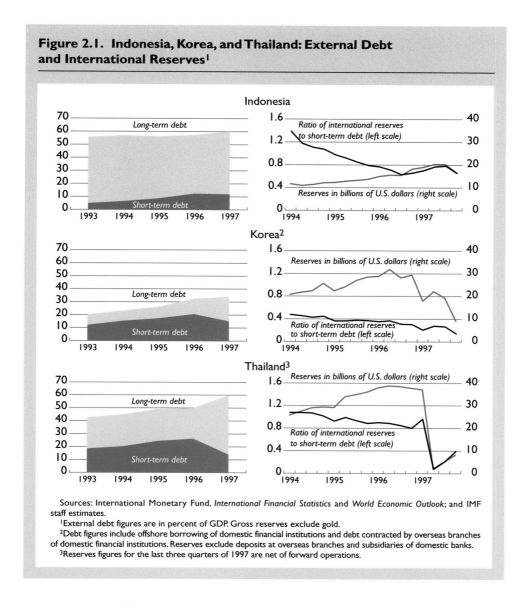

Figure 2.1. Indonesia, Korea, and Thailand: External Debt and International Reserves[1]

Sources: International Monetary Fund, *International Financial Statistics* and *World Economic Outlook*; and IMF staff estimates.

[1]External debt figures are in percent of GDP. Gross reserves exclude gold.

[2]Debt figures include offshore borrowing of domestic financial institutions and debt contracted by overseas branches of domestic financial institutions. Reserves exclude deposits at overseas branches and subsidiaries of domestic banks.

[3]Reserves figures for the last three quarters of 1997 are net of forward operations.

A key element of vulnerability associated with these inflows was the prevalence of unhedged short-term foreign currency borrowing. This was to some extent a prudential issue, as it was reflected in currency and maturity mismatches in the portfolios of banks and other financial institutions. It also implied aggregate vulnerability for these countries: as shown in Figure 2.1, while foreign debt as a percentage of GDP increased in all three countries (although only slightly in Indonesia), short-term debt rose considerably faster than total debt. Growth in short-term foreign liabilities also outpaced growth in available international reserves and created the potential for liquidity problems. Short-term debt exceeded gross international reserves in all three

countries for over two years prior to the onset of the crisis; in Korea, reserves had declined to about one-third of short-term debt by the end of 1996.[10]

The prevalence of unhedged foreign currency borrowing reflected various incentives that had free play

---

[10]At the same time, gross reserves were a poor indicator of available international liquidity given the magnitude of liabilities set against these reserves (many appearing off-balance sheet). Of particular importance in Thailand were forward contracts outstanding; in Korea, reserves were also lent to commercial banks via a special fund, as discussed below. (The latter reserves, however, are excluded from the figures presented in Figure 2.1.) These components were significant mainly in 1997. As data on usable reserves and comprehensive data on short-term debt were available only in the wake of the crisis, the detailed picture presented in Figure 2.1 was only known after the crisis erupted.

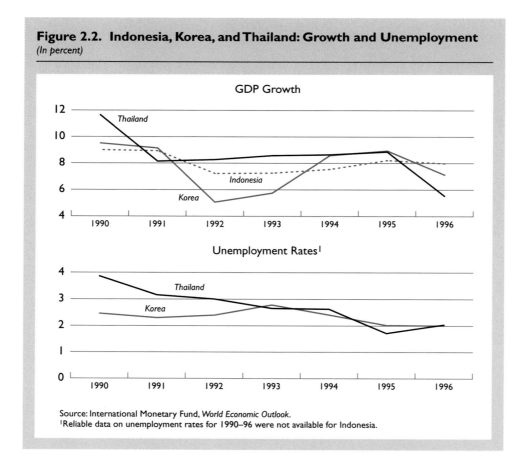

Figure 2.2. Indonesia, Korea, and Thailand: Growth and Unemployment
(In percent)

GDP Growth

Unemployment Rates[1]

Source: International Monetary Fund, *World Economic Outlook*.
[1]Reliable data on unemployment rates for 1990–96 were not available for Indonesia.

in the context of a deregulated domestic financial environment with lax supervision. Domestic interest rates that were above foreign rates,[11] together with a lack of exchange rate variability,[12] provided an incentive for borrowing in foreign exchange, most of which was unhedged. Borrowers may have underestimated the risks associated with foreign currency exposure and shunned the cost of hedging such exposure, which would have raised the cost of foreign borrowing close to domestic interest rates.[13] Lenders, for their part, may have ignored the fact that exchange rate risk for their debtors meant credit risk for them. Short-term foreign borrowing was also encouraged by the governments through the provision of explicit or implicit guarantees, and in Thailand was even institu-

tionalized and subsidized through the creation of the Bangkok International Bank Facility (BIBF)—a tax-exempt entity specialized in short-term borrowing from abroad and on-lending in the domestic market.

Macroeconomic Considerations

The financial vulnerabilities discussed above had been accumulating for some time, but became particularly problematic as macroeconomic conditions began to worsen. Following strong growth in 1994–95, economic activity in the three countries slowed in 1996 (Figure 2.2),[14] and overcapacities built up during the preceding investment boom (particularly in Korea) became increasingly evident. In Korea and Thailand, the deceleration in production was more pronounced and led to increases in unemployment rates, while in Indonesia the economy continued to operate at close to its productive capacity.

[11]This was particularly the case as regards yen rates, given Japan's close trade and financial ties with the region.
[12]The nominal exchange rate was essentially pegged to the U.S. dollar in Thailand, and depreciated in a reasonably predictable manner in Indonesia. In Korea, exchange rate policy sought to keep the won broadly stable in real effective terms.
[13]At the same time, global financial markets apparently did not put full confidence in the exchange rate peg, as indicated by the premium of domestic currency over dollar interest rates.

[14]For a detailed description of macroeconomic developments in the region prior to the crisis, see International Monetary Fund (1997).

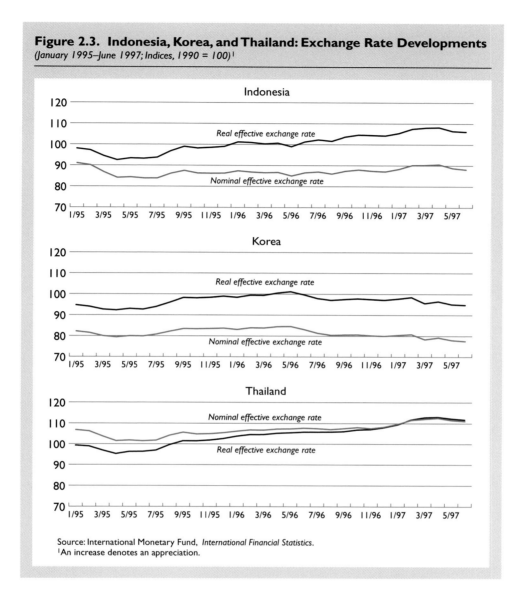

Figure 2.3. Indonesia, Korea, and Thailand: Exchange Rate Developments
(January 1995–June 1997; Indices, 1990 = 100)[1]

Indonesia

Korea

Thailand

Source: International Monetary Fund, *International Financial Statistics*.
[1]An increase denotes an appreciation.

The slowdown in output growth reflected a marked deceleration of export growth against the background of weakening demand in partner countries and modest real effective appreciations,[15] which in Indonesia and Thailand led to a fall in export market shares (Figures 2.3 and 2.4). In general, inflation was relatively low in all three countries during the 1990s.

In addition to weakening export growth, the three countries were affected—to different extents—by the sharp decline in prices of key export commodities, such as semiconductors. As a result, export revenues fell in Korea and Thailand, and grew only modestly in Indonesia. Current account imbalances remained large (Thailand) or widened significantly (Korea), as high domestic investment continued to outstrip national saving.

The fiscal situation in all three countries was apparently sound for many years prior to the crisis (although the implicit liabilities associated with

---

[15]The strengthening of the U.S. dollar vis-à-vis the Japanese yen and other major currencies since 1995 may have been another important factor affecting competitiveness in the crisis countries, whose currencies were more or less formally linked to the dollar. Some authors (Fernald and others, 1998) have examined the role of the large devaluation of China's official exchange rate in early 1994. However, the effective depreciation of the renmimbi at the time was relatively modest as most exchange transactions were already being carried out at the more depreciated (and unchanged swap) market rate.

Figure 2.4. Indonesia, Korea, and Thailand: Competitiveness Indicators

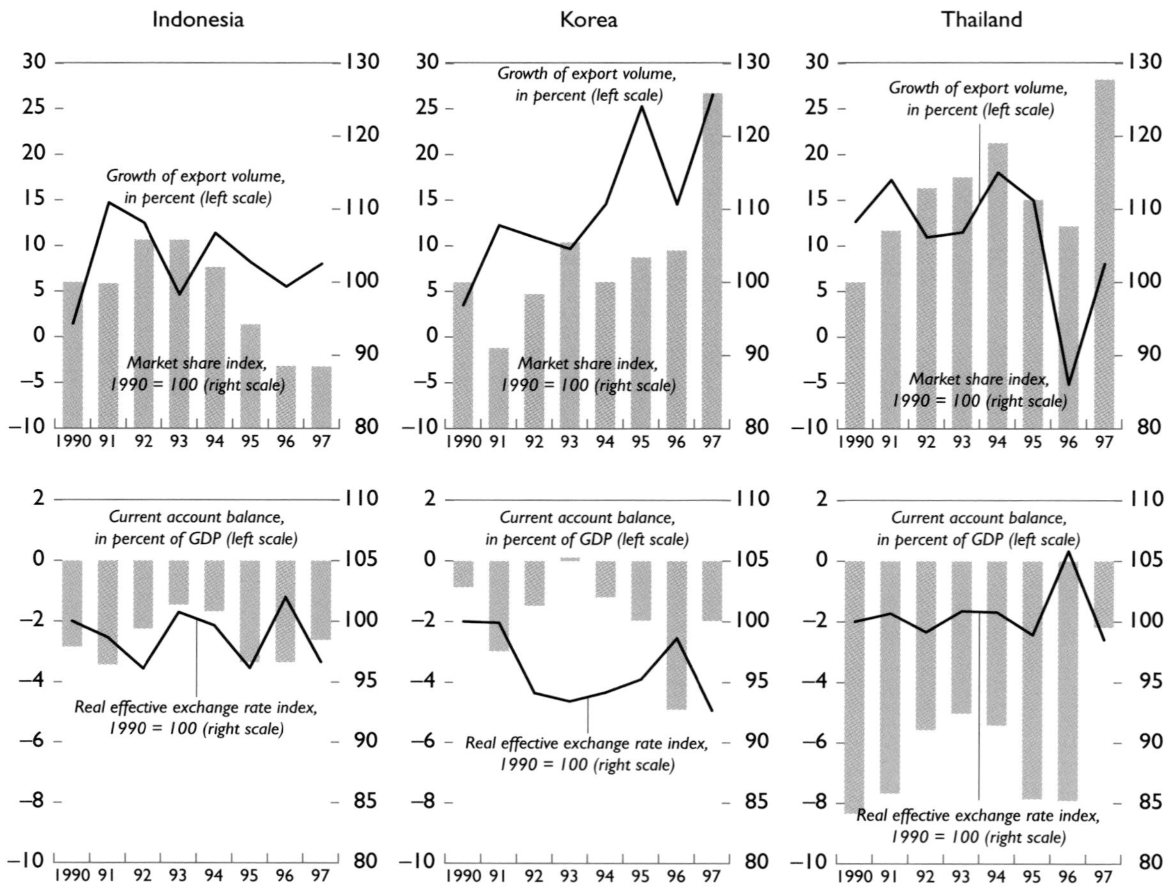

Sources: International Monetary Fund, *World Economic Outlook*; and IMF staff estimates.

government guarantees to weak financial institutions imply that these positions were weaker than they appeared). Both Korea and Indonesia ran surpluses prior to the crisis, following small deficits at the beginning of the 1990s (Figure 2.5). In Thailand, significant surpluses were recorded every year from 1990 through 1996. Prudent fiscal policies combined with high rates of economic growth led to rapidly declining public debt ratios in all three countries: at the end of 1996, government debt amounted to about 25 percent of GDP in Indonesia, and less than 10 percent in Korea and Thailand.

Monetary policies helped fuel the expansion during the 1990s with rapid money and credit creation.

Growth in total domestic credit considerably exceeded nominal GDP growth in all three countries and was particularly strong in 1993–94 (Figure 2.6). Given lax banking supervision, these surges in credit growth were liable to result in a deterioration in the average quality of banks' portfolios.

Asset Price Deflation and Bank Failures

Declining asset prices provided one of the earliest signs of trouble in the region. During 1996, stock prices (in domestic currency terms) fell by more than 20 percent in Korea and by almost one-

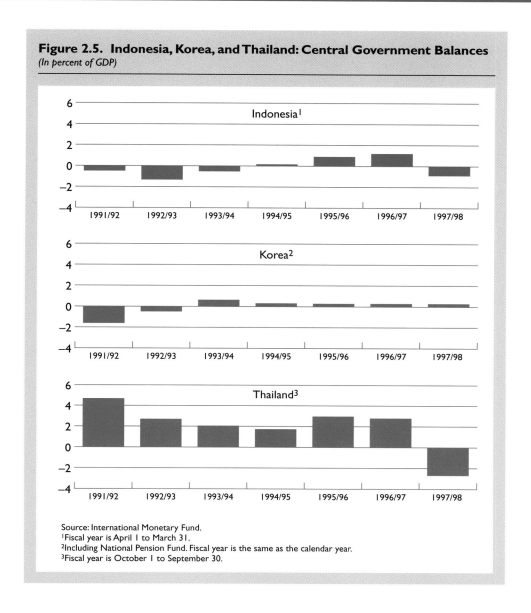

Figure 2.5. Indonesia, Korea, and Thailand: Central Government Balances
(In percent of GDP)

Source: International Monetary Fund.
[1]Fiscal year is April 1 to March 31.
[2]Including National Pension Fund. Fiscal year is the same as the calendar year.
[3]Fiscal year is October 1 to September 30.

third in Thailand (Figure 2.7). The decline continued in Thailand in early 1997; in Korea, it was temporarily interrupted in the first half of the year but continued in the second half. In Indonesia, stock prices increased through mid-1997, but fell dramatically in the aftermath of the Thai crisis.[16] In addition, property prices dropped significantly, particularly in Thailand and (after the crisis broke) in Indonesia.[17]

The declines in stock and property prices and the slowdown of economic activity reinforced each other,[18] aggravated the stock imbalances, and led to a self-perpetuating process of bankruptcies and bank failures in all three countries. In Indonesia, a run on the deposits of Lippo Bank in November 1995 and the support given by Bank Indonesia to two ailing banks in 1996 brought attention to the

---

[16]Earnings, on the other hand, grew slightly in 1996 but fell in late 1997. Movements in prices went beyond changes in underlying earnings.

[17]Inflation-adjusted residential property prices fell by almost 50 percent between end-1991 and end-1997 in Thailand; by about

one-third between late 1992 and mid-1997 in Indonesia; and by about one-fourth between mid-1990 and end-1997 in Korea (Bank for International Settlements, 1998, p. 140).

[18]Declining asset prices depressed economic activity through negative wealth effects on domestic demand, while the deteriorating outlook for growth put pressure on asset prices.

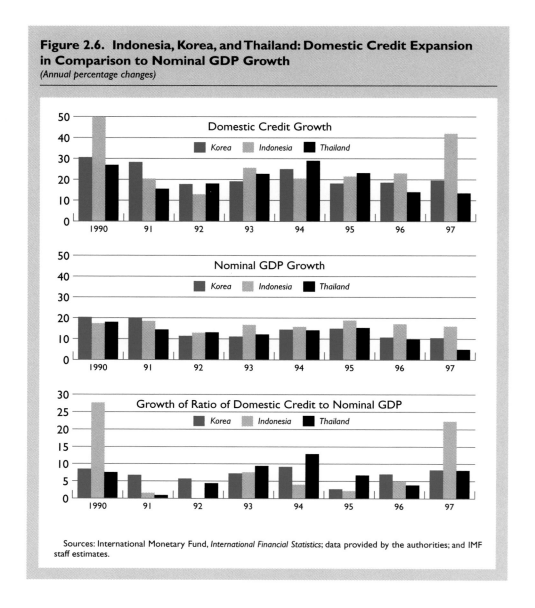

Figure 2.6. Indonesia, Korea, and Thailand: Domestic Credit Expansion in Comparison to Nominal GDP Growth
(Annual percentage changes)

Sources: International Monetary Fund, *International Financial Statistics*; data provided by the authorities; and IMF staff estimates.

fragile state of the banking sector, which had expanded at an extraordinary pace in the wake of banking sector liberalization in the late 1980s. In Korea several of the largest *chaebol* posted losses in 1996 and 6 of the top 30 went bankrupt in 1997 before the crisis broke. This weakened the already fragile situation of several commercial and merchant banks and led to increasing difficulties in external financing. In Thailand, Thai-owned commercial banks reported a significant increase in nonperforming loans in late 1996 and there was a run on the deposits of the Bangkok Bank of Commerce in May 1997. These tremors in the financial sector, together with the loss of foreign exchange reserves, culminated in a funding crisis that led to the collapse of the exchange rate regime.

References

Adams, Charles, Donald J. Mathieson, Garry Schinasi, and Bankim Chadha, 1998, *International Capital Markets: Developments, Prospects, and Key Policy Issues*, World Economic and Financial Surveys (Washington, International Monetary Fund).

Bank for International Settlements, 1998, *68th Annual Report* (Basle).

Berg, Andrew, forthcoming, "The Asian Crisis: Causes, Policy Responses, and Outcomes," IMF Working Paper (Washington: International Monetary Fund).

Figure 2.7. Indonesia, Korea, and Thailand: Stock Market Prices

(Domestic currency indices; January 1996 = 100)

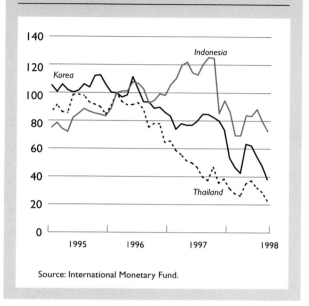

Source: International Monetary Fund.

Corsetti, Giancarlo, Paolo Pesenti, and Nouriel Roubini, 1998, "What Caused the Asian Currency and Financial Crisis?" (unpublished; New York: New York University).

Diamond, Douglas W., and Philip H. Dybvig, 1983, "Bank Runs, Deposit Insurance, and Liquidity," *Journal of Political Economy,* Vol. 91 (June), pp. 401–19.

Dooley, Michael P., 1997, "A Model of Crises in Emerging Markets," NBER Working Paper No. 6300 (Cambridge, Massachusetts: National Bureau of Economic Research).

Fernald, John, Hali Edison, and Prakash Loungani, 1998, "Was China the First Domino? Assessing Links Between Asia and the Rest of Emerging Asia," International Finance Discussion Paper No. 604 (Washington: Board of Governors of the Federal Reserve System).

Goldstein, Morris, 1998, *The Asian Financial Crisis: Causes, Cures, and Systemic Implications* (Washington: Institute for International Economics).

International Monetary Fund, 1997, *World Economic Outlook, December 1997: A Survey by the Staff of the International Monetary Fund,* World Economic and Financial Surveys (Washington).

Krugman, Paul, 1998, "What Happened to Asia?" (unpublished; Cambridge, Massachusetts: Massachusetts Institute of Technology).

Obstfeld, Maurice, 1996, "Models of Currency Crises with Self-Fulfilling Features," *European Economic Review,* Vol. 40 (April), pp. 1037–47.

Radelet, Steven, and Jeffrey D. Sachs, 1998, "The East Asian Financial Crisis: Diagnosis, Remedies, Prospects," *Brookings Papers on Economic Activity:1,* Brookings Institution, pp. 1–90.

III   Program Design

Timothy Lane

Basic Strategy

The policy response to the Asian crisis needed to be adapted to the distinctive features of the crisis. Understanding of the nature of the crisis was less clear when the programs were being formulated than it is now with the benefit of hindsight, but some broad aspects of the situation were apparent from the start. In contrast to the situations in many other countries with IMF-supported programs, the currency crises in East Asia did not reflect substantial fiscal imbalances. Rather, the proximate cause was a liquidity crisis, which called for a large financing package together with other steps intended to restore confidence and catalyze private capital flows alongside the financial support provided by the IMF and the official community more generally. But, at a deeper level, the origins of the crisis lay in serious vulnerabilities in banking and corporate sectors: including exchange and regulatory regimes that encouraged short-term foreign currency exposure, and stock imbalances within these countries, were problematic in conjunction with the volatility of short-term capital flows and external shocks—most notably terms of trade deteriorations and slowing growth of export markets. The programs therefore featured structural reforms that had few precedents in depth and breadth.

In these circumstances, and given the inherent uncertainties involved, the programs incorporated a three-pronged response. First, structural reforms were intended to build confidence and staunch capital outflows. Second, macroeconomic policies were to be adjusted: in order to ease the private sector's burden of adjustment to the capital outflows, a modest fiscal tightening was planned; and efforts to limit capital flight were to be buttressed by tightened monetary policies. Third, large financing packages were provided to help restore confidence.

The central focus of the structural reforms was to reestablish the financial systems on a sound footing, rectifying preexisting weaknesses that had been compounded by the crisis itself. Other reforms were intended to put in place conditions for a sustainable resumption of growth.

Fiscal policy was ascribed a rather modest role in these programs, since at the time the programs were formulated, the need for external current account adjustment was seen as relatively small (except in Thailand). Fiscal policies were thus intended to provide only limited support for a modest current account adjustment, mainly by reversing an initial deterioration of fiscal positions and covering the prospective carrying costs of financial sector restructuring.

Monetary policy was assigned the role of countering downward pressure on exchange rates to contain the overshooting of the exchange rate beyond the degree of real exchange rate adjustment needed in light of underlying fundamentals. It was thought that, if unchecked, such overshooting could trigger depreciation-inflation spirals; in addition, excessive depreciations could elicit corresponding exchange rate movements in competitor countries, with detrimental effects on the system as a whole. Moreover, continued depreciation imposed substantial burdens on both corporate and banking sectors, which were already suffering from their overexposure to foreign-currency-denominated liabilities.

The structural reform strategy in the programs was exceptionally comprehensive and went to the heart of the weaknesses in financial systems and in governance that were seen to be at the root of the crisis. Such a comprehensive strategy was needed principally because of the interdependence of reforms in different areas. For instance, if macroeconomic stabilization had been attempted without dealing with weak and insolvent financial institutions, monetary policy would have been thwarted by the need for liquidity support to these financial institutions, while fiscal positions would have been burdened by mounting liabilities associated with pervasive government guarantees; but dealing with weak institutions without establishing sound ground rules for financial supervision and regulation would have invited a repetition of the crisis; and financial restructuring would have made little progress without effective mechanisms for working out corporate debt, which in turn required the establishment of effective bankruptcy procedures. For this reason, the credibility of the programs required moving quickly across a broad (and, in some areas, uncharted) front. In keeping with responsibilities among the international financial institutions, the World Bank and the Asian Development Bank were extensively involved in formulating and implementing these reforms.

Exchange Rates

Another key element of the programs supported by the IMF was the decision to permit exchange rates to continue to float—part of the initial response of the authorities in all three countries to the pressures that had emerged—rather than readjusting the pegs to rates deemed to be defensible and consistent with medium-term fundamentals. Floating exchange rates removed the main anchor for expectations, without putting anything comparable in its place.[1] Floating may have introduced an additional element of instability into the mix: given that countries in the region trade heavily with one another and compete in many of the same export markets, any depreciation of one currency would put downward pressure on the others. Arguably, the resulting spiral of depreciations might have been avoided—or at least slowed down—by pegging the currencies. More generally, as discussed below, given the high exposure of these countries' residents to exchange rate movements, depreciation had side effects that could be destabilizing: it swelled domestic money stocks (especially in Indonesia, where foreign currency deposits were particularly large); it weakened fiscal positions (by raising debt-servicing costs and costs of food subsidies and lowering corporate tax receipts from foreign-currency-indebted companies); and it deepened the problems of insolvency in banking sectors and nonbank corporations.

However, pegging these currencies in the midst of the crisis would have been difficult—if not impossible—for several reasons. It would have required a commitment of the authorities to use monetary policy unstintingly to defend their currencies—even if that required raising interest rates to ruinous levels. The reserves needed to defend the currencies were depleted (in Thailand in net terms; in Korea in usable terms); replenishing them to a level adequate to defend a new peg could have required financing on a scale that would not have been available. Pegging also would have carried the risk of losing more credibility by having to abandon a new peg under market pressure—as had happened with the

Mexican devaluation of December 1994. Another concern about repegging was that a rate that could have been defended against short-run market pressures may have been much too depreciated to be appropriate to lock in for the medium term. Moreover, the first failed attempts to deal with exchange market pressures also did not set the stage for credible action to defend the currencies. Thus, although at an earlier stage a more orderly adjustment might well have been possible as well as desirable, in the heat of the crisis there was seen to be no practical alternative to floating.

In the event, exchange rates depreciated considerably after the inception of the programs, and far overshot levels estimated to be consistent with medium-term fundamentals.[2] Monetary policy sought to lean against the wind to dampen the overshooting of nominal exchange rates and avert depreciation-inflation spirals. There were no preannounced targets, but there were understandings about exchange rates, which were frequently revised in response to the changing market conditions.

References

Feldstein, Martin, 1998, "Refocusing the IMF," *Foreign Affairs,* Vol. 77 (March–April), pp. 20–33.

Isard, Peter, and Hamid Faruqee, 1998, *Exchange Rate Assessment: Extensions of the Macroeconomic Balance Approach,* IMF Occasional Paper No. 167 (Washington: International Monetary Fund).

Schadler, Susan, Adam Bennett, Maria Carkovic, Louis Dicks-Mireaux, Mauro Mecagni, James H.J. Morsink, and Miguel A. Savastano, 1995, *IMF Conditionality: Experience Under Stand-By and Extended Arrangements,* IMF Occasional Paper No. 128 (Washington: International Monetary Fund).

Stiglitz, Joseph, 1998, "Knowledge for Development: Economic Science, Economic Policy, and Economic Advice," paper prepared for the Annual World Bank Conference on Development Economics, April 20–21 (Washington).

---

[1]As will be discussed below, uncertainties were probably compounded by irresolution and a lack of transparency in monetary policy implementation in the early periods of the programs.

---

[2]Such assessments are based on a comparison of a country's underlying current account that would prevail if output were at potential and once lags have worked themselves out with a norm for its appropriate medium-term current account (see Isard and Faruqee, 1998). Applying this framework to the Asian crisis countries is particularly imprecise because of difficulties in estimating (1) output gaps in economies undergoing massive structural reforms and dislocation associated with the crisis; (2) the implications of prevailing exchange rates once lagged effects have worked themselves out in the face of very large exchange rate movements; and (3) the basis for establishing an appropriate norm for the current account given massive (but probably not permanent) changes in external financing flows. However, such estimates confirm that, for a range of assumptions, exchange rate depreciations far overshot any initial misalignment.

IV   Program Financing and Market Reactions

Timothy Lane and Marianne Schulze-Ghattas

The sufficiency of financing is key to the viability of any IMF-supported program. The Asian crisis countries' estimated financing needs were heavily dominated by the capital account and in particular the assumed rollover rate on short-term foreign debt.[1] The size of the short-term liabilities was such that it was essential that creditors roll over at least a good part of their positions. Inducing them to do so required persuading them that the programs would work, showing that there was enough official money available to make them work, and suggesting that pulling money out unilaterally would not be in their longer-term interests—a particularly difficult task when dealing with short-term, fixed-value credits.

In each of the programs (but particularly in Indonesia and Korea) very large official financing packages, together with sound economic policies, were intended to restore confidence and limit private capital outflows. However, the programs were not initially successful in restoring confidence, and private capital outflows far exceeded program projections. Several factors contributed to weak confidence, including hesitant program implementation, political uncertainties, and other factors casting doubt on the authorities' ownership of the programs, the revelation of market-sensitive information, problems with the coverage of government guarantees, and uncertainties surrounding the financing packages.

In the event, the financing available was inadequate to protect the programs from a failure to restore market confidence quickly. This suggests two main alternatives. One would have been a larger official financing package (or greater front-loading of the packages), although this was limited by resource constraints and moral hazard concerns. A second would have been earlier concerted involvement of the private sector; such action could have been considered at an earlier stage in these countries, but there are no straightforward mechanisms to assure such involvement, and the attempt, at a moment of nervousness across the emerging market countries, could have increased the risk of contagion. The experience, which is discussed below, underscores the importance of ongoing work on international financial architecture, including more effective ways of involving the private sector in the resolution of financial crisis.

Official Financing and Program Projections

The approach taken in these cases involved trying to strike a delicate balance, with a promise of official financing that, although large, was far from sufficient to constitute a guarantee of external liabilities. It was hoped that this commitment, together with firm policy implementation in line with the programs, would elicit a spontaneous response from private market participants such that the official financing package would not be needed, at least not in full. The alternatives would have been to withhold support or initiate a more formal approach to private creditors (to the extent that they could be identified and organized) to keep their money in place.

Given the size and openness of the countries involved and thus the enormous potential volume of capital outflows, the amount of financing provided in these packages had few precedents (Table 4.1).[2] In addition to the financing provided by the IMF itself, large amounts of bilateral and other multilateral (the World Bank and the Asian Development Bank) support were pledged, which exceeded the IMF's support. In Thailand, bilateral funds amounting to $10.5 billion were part of the package and have been disbursed in step with the IMF's resources. In Indonesia and Korea, a "second line of defense" was pledged by bilateral creditors, which, however, had not been disbursed as of October 1998.

---

[1]Current account imbalances were also important especially in Thailand, but in all three countries capital flows were a major element of variability in the external situation.

[2]By way of comparison, the financial support package for Mexico in early 1995 amounted to $50 billion, including $18 billion from the IMF.

Table 4.1. Official Financing

	In Billions of SDRs	In Billions of U.S. Dollars	In Percent of Annual GDP	In Percent of IMF Quota[1]
Indonesia[2]				
IMF	7,338	10.1	5	490
Asian Development Bank and World Bank		8.0	4	
Other		18.0	9	
Total package		36.1	17	
Korea				
IMF	15,500	21.1	5	1,938
Asian Development Bank and World Bank		14.2	3	
Other		23.1	5	
Total package		58.4	13	
Thailand				
IMF	2,900	4.0	3	505
Asian Development Bank and World Bank		2.7	2	
Other		10.5	7	
Total package		17.2	12	

[1]Duration of original arrangements was 36 months for Indonesia and Korea and 34 months for Thailand.
[2]Original financing package, not including augmentations since July 1998.

Large as this official financing was, it would have been sufficient to support the programs in Indonesia and Korea only on the assumption that they would elicit a broadly positive response on the part of private markets, especially in the initial phase of the programs.[3] It was known, however, that there was a substantial risk that private capital outflows would turn out larger than assumed. If this risk materialized and the program financing thus turned out to be inadequate, the perceptions that had led investors to panic in the first place would be confirmed, leading into a vicious circle. This risk was compounded by the fact that much of the external debt outstanding was of private corporations and banks: this meant that external creditors were less easily reassured by the IMF's and other commitments of official resources—which left these creditors with significant uncertainties about individual debtors' solvency and ability to finance the purchases of foreign currency needed to service their debts.

Given that unpredictable private capital outflows were central to program financing, an obvious question is whether more direct action should have been taken at an earlier stage to limit these outflows by attempting a rescheduling of private external debt (Box 4.1 reviews attempts to involve the private sector in the three countries). Programs in Korea and Indonesia were formulated without any advance agreement to restructure debt. Such agreements were discussed with major private external creditors only at a later stage. Korea brought about an effective standstill on bank debt in late December 1997 and made a provisional agreement with its private bank creditors in late January 1998. Indonesia concluded an agreement with private creditors in late June. In Thailand, however, the authorities at the outset received certain assurances and indications regarding maintenance of credit lines of foreign banks resident in the country.[4] Would it have been desirable—if it had been possible in the limited time available—for the IMF to have exerted pressure to bring about a refinancing or rescheduling beforehand in the other countries? This would likely have lengthened and complicated program negotiations by turning them into (at least) a three-way process, and (particularly in Korea)

---

[3]The assumption was that a virtuous circle would be generated by the knowledge that official financing would be available.

[4]These assurances, involving credit lines of $19 billion, were received at a meeting with Japanese creditor banks in mid-August 1997. Some uncertainties remained, however, regarding short-term credit lines to Thai banks ($11 billion).

Box 4.1. Involving Private Sector Creditors

In all three countries, uncertainty about the rollover of short-term foreign debt presented a major risk to the programs. The initial focus was on the restoration of confidence through convincing packages of policies and official financing to induce private creditors to maintain their exposure voluntarily. At different stages, more direct action was also taken to involve private creditors in the closing of financing gaps. The form and timing of this involvement reflected the specific circumstances of each country.

Thailand

In Thailand, steps were taken at the start of the program to encourage the rollover of a significant part of maturing short-term debt. These steps were facilitated by the fact that some two-thirds of total short-term debt outstanding prior to the program was owed by foreign bank branches and subsidiaries, mainly of Japanese banks.

In August 1997, shortly before the Stand-By Arrangement was approved by the IMF's Executive Board, the Thai authorities received assurances and indications that credit lines of foreign banks resident in Thailand, the bulk of which involved Japanese banks on the creditor and debtor side, would be maintained. As a result, rollover rates for short-term obligations of foreign banks in Thailand remained high through April 1998, but subsequently declined, mainly reflecting problems at home of Japanese creditor banks. The rollover of short-term obligations of Thai banks and corporations meanwhile declined sharply in early 1998, but recovered by midyear.

Korea

In Korea, the financial sector accounted for the bulk of short-term foreign liabilities, but unlike in Thailand, most of the short-term debt (over half at the end of November 1997) was owed by domestic financial institutions (including their overseas branches and subsidiaries) and the geographical distribution of creditor banks was more dispersed. Efforts to involve private sector creditors were thus likely to be more complicated.

When the original Stand-By Arrangement with Korea was approved by the IMF's Executive Board on December 4, 1997, it was expected that the program, combined with the announcement of a large financing package, would turn around market sentiment. Talks with private sector creditors were not envisaged.

In late December, however, with rollover of short-term debt down sharply and usable official reserves effectively depleted notwithstanding the injection of about $10 billion from the IMF, discussions with creditor banks became critical. Talks in Japan, the United States, and Europe led to voluntary cooperative understandings on the maintenance of interbank credit lines to Korea through end-March 1998. At the same time, discussions on a framework for voluntary restructuring of short-term debt were initiated. A detailed debt-monitoring system was set up to track daily rollover rates. In early January, rollover rates rose significantly.

On January 28, 1998, the Korean authorities reached an agreement in principle with a committee of foreign banks on a voluntary restructuring of the short-term debt of 33 commercial and specialized banks (including their overseas branches) as well as certain merchant banks. The eligible debt, amounting to some $24 billion, covered interbank obligations and short-term loans maturing during 1998.

The debt-restructuring agreement was signed on March 31, 1998, with 134 creditor banks from 32 countries tendering loans and deposits amounting to $21.8 billion. The original obligations were exchanged for government-guaranteed debt of one-year maturity at 225 basis points over the London interbank offered rate (LIBOR) (17 percent of total), two-year maturity at 250 basis points over LIBOR (45 percent of total), and

---

there was not much time before a moratorium and/or exchange controls would have had to be activated. Greater assurances that the countries would be adequately financed might have been worth some additional delay. On the other hand, there was concern that an approach that was perceived as "heavy-handed" could both precipitate greater capital flight from the countries immediately concerned and unsettle conditions for market access by other countries both in and beyond the region—countries that were themselves already under some pressure from the market uncertainties created by the Asian crisis. These issues are among the thorniest being addressed in current discussions of the international financial architecture.

Market Reactions

In any case, the programs were vulnerable to adverse market reactions, and those reactions turned out to be far less favorable than hoped—especially in Indonesia and Korea, with the situation in both cases sliding into funding crises.[5] As a result, private

---

[5]By way of comparison, during the Mexican crisis of 1994–95, the announcement of several international credit packages in January and February 1995 failed to restore confidence, and the peso continued to depreciate. However, the announcement of a strengthened fiscal plan on March 9, 1995, and the subsequent authorization from the United States to draw the first US$3 billion of a loan agreed a few days earlier, had a substantially favorable effect on

three-year maturity at 275 basis points over LIBOR (38 percent of total). As a result of the debt restructuring, Korea's short-term debt declined from $61 billion at end-March to $42 billion at end-April 1998.

Indonesia

The original Stand-By Arrangement with Indonesia, which was approved by the IMF's Executive Board on November 5, 1997, assumed that the official financing package, supplemented by part of Indonesia's own reserves, would be sufficient to cope even with a relatively large decline in the rollover of short-term debt. At the time, steps to restructure external obligations did not seem pressing. Moreover, with nearly half of total external debt (three-fourths of private external debt) owed by private corporations, efforts to involve private sector creditors were likely to be particularly complicated.

With the deepening of the crisis and continued depreciation of the rupiah in late 1997 and early 1998, however, the external debt of the private sector became an issue that had to be addressed. Talks with a steering committee of private bank creditors began in February 1998, followed by meetings in April (New York), May (Tokyo), and June (Frankfurt). A private external debt team set up by the authorities prepared and coordinated the negotiations with assistance from outside consultants and in collaboration with the IMF, the World Bank, and the Asian Development Bank. In addition, a system was established to monitor daily the rollover of short-term interbank credit lines.

On June 4, 1998, the Indonesian authorities reached an agreement with the steering committee of creditor banks on a multifaceted deal to support the restructuring of the external debt of the banking and corporate sectors. The agreement on interbank debt involved an offer to exchange short-, medium-, and long-term obligations maturing by end-March 1999 against new loans carrying a full dollar guarantee from Bank In-

donesia and maturities of one year (not more than 15 percent of the new loans) to four years (at least 10 percent of the new loans), with interest rates ranging form 275 to 350 basis points over LIBOR. Regarding trade credit, participating banks agreed to use their best effort to maintain, for the period of one year, aggregate credit to Indonesian banks at the level outstanding at end-April 1998.

The agreement on corporate debt provided a framework for the voluntary restructuring of external obligations of the corporate sector. It offered a government exchange guarantee to creditors and debtors who agreed to restructure their debt on the basis of certain minimum conditions (a three-year grace period and an eight-year maturity). A new government entity, the Indonesian Debt Restructuring Agency (INDRA), was to be established to operate the scheme, which was similar to the FICORCA scheme in Mexico. INDRA would not take on commercial risk but would ensure foreign payments to the creditor on the basis of rupiah payments received from the debtor, the latter being determined based on the most appreciated real exchange rate during a specified period.

Experience with the implementation of the June agreement has, so far, been mixed. By mid-October 1998, interbank obligations amounting to $2.9 billion had been exchanged; while this represented a very large proportion of the identified eligible debt, it was considerably lower than originally anticipated on the basis of preliminary estimates of eligible debt. Regarding trade credit, assurances equivalent to $2.7 billion have been received. Implementing the framework for corporate debt restructuring has proved time-consuming. However, with the establishment of INDRA in August 1998, complemented by a set of guidelines for debt workouts (Jakarta Initiative) and subsequent steps to set up the necessary legal framework, preparatory work is now largely complete. INDRA is promoting the program among creditor and debtor groups and intends to circulate the documentation shortly.

capital outflows were much larger (Box 4.2) and exchange rates much weaker than originally envisaged (Table 4.2).

Market reactions were less favorable than anticipated in the initial programs for several reasons: it took longer than expected to establish the credibility of economic policies, including in the structural area; most of the external debt was private, so that creditors needed to be assured not just of the country's but also of the individual debtor's ability to pay; and as the crises unfolded, investors became in-

creasingly aware of these countries' vulnerabilities, in particular the depth of problems in the banking and corporate sectors.

Establishing credibility—including reassuring foreign investors that private sector creditworthiness would be restored—was intrinsically difficult. For example, plans to recapitalize banks took considerable time to design in detail, let alone implement, and announced programs could only specify the broad outlines and discrete measures used as performance criteria. The outcome of such financial sector reform plans also depended on the authorities' commitment to implementation, and some early developments cast doubt on ownership of the programs. A degree of market skepticism was thus understandable.

---

confidence and the exchange rate appreciated by 20 percent against the U.S. dollar between then and end of April 1995.

Box 4.2. Projected Private Capital Flows in the Three Programs

Thailand

Excessively optimistic projections of private capital flows do not appear to have been a problem in Thailand at the outset; in fact, the outturn for 1997 was somewhat stronger than original program projections. This was in large part due to an informal understanding with foreign (mainly Japanese) banks with subsidiaries resident in Thailand that their lines of credit would be maintained. Average rollover rates were still very high in October 1997, but declined significantly in December 1997 and January 1998, reflecting a sharp drop in the rollover of obligations of Thai banks and corporations. Since then, average rollover rates have recovered, but capital flow projections for 1998 have been revised downward substantially since the first review.

	Original Program (8/97)	First Quarterly Review (11/97)	Second Quarterly Review (2/98)	Third Quarterly Review (5/98)	Fourth Quarterly Review (8/98)
	(In billions of U.S. dollars)				
1997 capital account balance[1]	−16.4	−17.9	−18.0	−15.8[2]	−14.8[2]
1998 capital account balance[1]	1.8	0.3	−14.3	−13.6	−18.1

[1]Excluding errors and omissions and official financing.
[2]Preliminary outcome.

Korea

In Korea, private capital outflows in late 1997 (mainly through the domestic banking system) turned out to be considerably larger than projected in the original program, with attendant strong pressures on the exchange rate. The original program assumed that the "bulk of the short-term debt will be rolled over." In the event, rollover rates declined sharply in December 1997, prompting discussions with private creditors at the end of the year, which were concluded on January 28, 1998. Nevertheless, further downward revisions to the capital account projections for 1998 were necessary at the time of the second review, mainly on account of trade financing difficulties experienced by small and medium-sized enterprises.

	Original Program (12/97)	First Quarterly Review (2/98)	Second Quarterly Review (5/98)	Third Quarterly Review (7/98)	Fourth Quarterly Review (11/98)
	(In billions of U.S. dollars)				
1997 capital account balance[1]	−11.1	−26.9	−27.5	−28.0[2]	−28.0[2]
1998 capital account balance[1]	3.3	−3.8	−11.0	−14.9	−16.0

[1]Including errors and omissions and excluding official financing.
[2]Preliminary outcome.

Indonesia

In Indonesia, the original program severely underestimated the extent of capital outflows in the initial phase of the program. Outflows from the stock market, which amounted to $5.5 billion in the last quarter of 1997, played a key role, together with low rollover rates of short-term debt. The need for an agreement with creditor banks became increasingly apparent in late January–early February 1998. Negotiations were protracted amidst uncertainty about the possibility of a unilateral pause in debt payments. An agreement was concluded in early June 1998, covering the restructuring of interbank debt, trade financing, and a framework for voluntary restructuring of corporate debt involving a government exchange guarantee scheme (INDRA).

	Original Program (11/97)	First Quarterly Review (4/98)	Second Quarterly Review (7/98)	Extended Arrangement (8/98)	First Review Under Extended Fund Facility (9/98)
	(In billions of U.S. dollars)				
4/97–3/98 capital account balance[1]	−0.5	−13.5	−10.8[2]	−10.8[2]	−10.8[2]
4/98–3/99 capital account balance[3]	0.9	−2.9	−6.2	−3.4	−1.4

[1]Including errors and omissions and official capital flows.
[2]Preliminary outcome.
[3]Including errors and omissions, official capital, and effect of rescheduling.

A lack of firm resolution in the implementation of macroeconomic policies also undermined credibility. The Indonesian authorities, for example, initially raised interest rates in line with the program but then rolled back the increase a week later. The Korean authorities likewise were reluctant to raise interest rates at the outset. More generally, the credibility of monetary policies was impaired in all three countries by the financial sector weaknesses that were seen by many to limit the authorities' scope to raise interest rates. Political uncertainties also played a major role—notably, in Korea, the presidential elections and the initial dis-

Table 4.2. Exchange Rate Assumptions

Country/Program Vintage	Date[1]	Prevailing Exchange Rate[2]	Projections[3]	
			1997[4]	1998[5]
Indonesia (rupiah/US$)				
Initial program	10/97	3,275	3,193	3,210
First review	4/98	8,325		5,915
Second review	6/98	10,525		10,545
Extended arrangement	8/98	13,000		10,564
First review	9/98	11,075		10,564
Second review	10/98	10,700		10,564
Korea (won/US$)				
Initial program	12/97	1,164	957	1,186
First quarterly review	2/98	1,525		1,426
Second quarterly review	5/98	1,336		1,417
Third quarterly review	8/98	1,230		1,440
Fourth quarterly review	11/98	1,319		1,425
Thailand (baht/US$)				
Initial program	8/97	32	...	32
First review	11/97	40	...	40
Second review	2/98	55		46
Third review	5/98	39		41
Fourth review	8/98	41		43
Memorandum items:				
Indonesia (rupiah/US$)				
End-1996	12/96	2,363		
Most depreciated rate	6/98	16,650		
Korea (won/US$)				
End-1996	12/96	841		
Most depreciated rate	12/97	1,963		
Thailand (baht/US$)				
End-1996	12/96	25.7		
Most depreciated rate	1/98	55.5		

[1]Dates when programs were negotiated.
[2]End-period exchange rate for month preceding date shown for program or review.
[3]Year average exchange rates.
[4]April 1997–March 1998 for Indonesia; calendar year for Korea.
[5]April 1998–March 1999 for Indonesia; October 1997–September 1998 for Thailand; and calendar year for Korea.

avowal of the program by the presidential candidates immediately after its acceptance by the government; and in Indonesia, conflicting signals from the regime regarding its commitment to the program. In Thailand, there were also some uncertainties as the government that negotiated the original program was a fragile coalition that eventually fell; a new, more stable coalition government was established only in November 1997. While political uncertainties were by no means unique to these countries—indeed, they are a salient element in many IMF-supported programs— they had a particular impact given the countries' vulnerabilities to international capital outflows.

Some other country-specific factors may also have contributed to the failure to reverse capital outflows. For instance, prior to the approval of Korea's

initial program with the IMF, the Bank of Korea established a facility to provide foreign currency refinancing to commercial banks. The interest rate was initially set at a small spread over the London interbank offered rate (LIBOR). One of the measures introduced in connection with the IMF-supported program was to widen this spread to 400 basis points over LIBOR (on December 4, 1997), seen at the time as a penalty rate. In the event, market interest rates facing Korean banks at the time turned out to be much higher, so the rate charged on this facility continued to entail a subsidy. The banks made extensive use of this facility, channeling the funds to their offshore subsidiaries that were having difficulties rolling over their foreign currency liabilities. Such flows to offshore subsidiaries accounted for a large share of Korea's capital outflows during December 1997. The rate charged on refinance was subsequently raised (to 1,000 basis points on December 23, 1997) to bring it into line with market rates.

Another factor that influenced market reactions to the programs, by both domestic and foreign investors, was the coverage of government guarantees. This was a particularly controversial factor in Indonesia: when the government closed 16 banks in November 1997, it announced guarantees on deposits in those banks that (in line with the IMF's advice) covered only deposits up to the equivalent of about $5,000. This signaled to large depositors who held the bulk of deposits that their funds—at least those in private banks—might not be repaid should any more banks be closed. Moreover, no announcement was made regarding the protection that would be provided depositors—beyond that presumed to apply to the deposit liabilities of the state banks—in the event of any subsequent bank closures. This policy toward guarantees, at a time when banking weaknesses were widespread, with public knowledge that many other private banks were in as bad a condition as the 16 that had been closed, was an important factor contributing to bank runs. There is no doubt that some banks needed to be closed (see Section VIII below) and it is quite possible that closing a larger number of banks in this early phase of the program might have induced more confidence in the banking sector. However, the policy regarding guarantees now appears to have been ill-advised—notwithstanding good economic reasons in principle for limiting depositor protection. Indeed, in late January 1998, this policy was modified, with a full guarantee issued on all bank liabilities for two years. Anecdotal evidence that there was little public awareness of *any* deposit guarantee, and that many depositors who participated in the bank runs had deposits below the maximum covered, suggests, however, that other factors may also have contributed to the bank runs.

The markets also became more aware of the weaknesses of the authorities' financial positions as the programs unfolded. In part, this was a reflection of the fact that (especially in Korea and Thailand) the authorities turned to the IMF quite late, and only after exhausting their reserves. A related issue was the revelation of information associated with the programs themselves. Notably, in Korea, the staff report was leaked over the Internet, informing market participants that "usable reserves" were at a perilously low level in relation to maturing short-term debt (since a substantial portion of Korea's reported reserves were actually illiquid claims on overseas branches of Korean banks). Similarly, the Thai authorities, in the midst of the crisis, were required to release data on the central bank's forward foreign exchange positions that revealed the weakness of the country's reserve position. This was intended as a step toward greater transparency, in line

with the IMF-supported program, but its timing weakened the impact on confidence that the announcement of the program could have had.

Another element of market uncertainty surrounded the official financing packages. Of particular relevance are the "second lines of defense," which were pledged by bilateral creditors in Indonesia and Korea but had not been disbursed as of October 1998. The precise terms and conditions under which the second line would be disbursed were never clearly specified. If the "virtuous circle" assumed in the IMF-supported programs had materialized, the second line would not have been needed; however, the uncertainties about their availability may have influenced market participants in their decision to continue their exit—in effect testing the second lines of defense.

A related issue is that IMF and other official financial support was "phased"—that is, disbursed in tranches at the outset of the program and on completion of successive reviews, conditional on the program's remaining on track; although in the Asian crisis countries, total financing was unprecedentedly large and was heavily front-loaded compared with other programs. Such phasing is a standard feature of IMF programs, aimed at providing support to meet balance of payments needs while safeguarding the IMF's resources and maintaining the authorities' incentives for continued implementation of the program. Choosing the appropriate schedule of disbursement involves a trade-off between these considerations and considerations related to the market's uncertainty about the availability of such resources: phasing implies that the full amount of the financing package is not available to the authorities from the start and there always remains the possibility that later tranches will not be disbursed as scheduled, in the event that the programs go off track.

The communication of the rationale and substance of the programs may also have influenced the reaction to the programs, by both market participants and the general public. Several weaknesses in communication were apparent in the initial Asian crisis programs. One shortcoming in all three countries at the outset was the absence of an effective government economic spokesperson, available to explain the program to the public, underscore the government's support for it, and respond to public concerns as events unfolded. The many public statements of the IMF in support of the policies followed by Indonesia and Korea before (and right after) their currencies collapsed did little to restore confidence. Even if many of the miscommunications that occurred were beyond the IMF's control—and indeed, this element improved significantly, especially with the establishment of new governments in Korea and Thailand—they gave impetus to the efforts under way to improve communication about IMF-supported programs.

V   Macroeconomic Environment

Timothy Lane and Steven Phillips

The Asian crisis plunged the countries affected into deep recessions. As of October 1998, real GDP was estimated to decline in 1998 by 7 percent in Korea, 8 percent in Thailand, and 15 percent in Indonesia.[1] The slowdown in economic activity was dramatically different from that assumed in formulating the programs, and its magnitude, once appreciated, prompted revisions in economic policies.

Corresponding to the economic slump were massive corrections in external current accounts. The corrections were especially large in Korea (with a current account adjustment of 15 percentage points of GDP) and Thailand (12 percentage points), but even in Indonesia it is expected to be substantial (over 4 percentage points). The slump was, to a large extent, forced on these economies by the withdrawal of foreign capital and flight of domestic capital: the reversal of capital flows necessitated large current account adjustments that were then brought about by huge currency depreciations and precipitous drops in domestic demand, especially fixed investment. The ability of depreciations to stimulate exports may have been limited due to concurrent depreciations in several countries in the region and deteriorating economic prospects in some major trading partners, including Japan.[2] At the same time, given the unhedged exposures of domestic firms and financial institutions, the depreciations had devastating balance sheet effects that, along with worsening consumer and business confidence, were a major reason for collapses in domestic demand.

The IMF, like most observers, misread the extent of the recession. This was largely a reflection of the fact that, as in all IMF-supported programs, macroeconomic projections were predicated on the success of the programs, including the restoration of confidence. Moreover, the IMF and the authorities appear to have erred on the side of optimism in part because of concerns that realistically pessimistic forecasts would have exacerbated the situation further—but the resulting large revisions in projections were detrimental to credibility.

This section first discusses the nature of the economic slowdown and the reasons for its severity. It draws, in part, on analysis in other studies, including the October 1998 *World Economic Outlook* (International Monetary Fund, 1998). It then considers why the initial program projections were so far off the mark.

Output Decline and Its Causes

In all three countries, the output decline was associated with a collapse in domestic demand, while net external demand expanded (Figure 5.1). Domestic expenditure declined in 1998 by much more than the decline in GDP: by 25 percent in Korea, 18 percent in Thailand, and 17 percent in Indonesia. This divergence corresponded to the large adjustments in external current accounts that took place. In Indonesia, the decline in domestic demand was much closer to that in output, reflected in a proportionately smaller current account adjustment.

In all three countries, the central reason for the decline in domestic demand was a precipitous drop in investment expenditure (Figure 5.2). Gross fixed investment fell by more than one-fourth in Korea and Thailand, and by more than half in Indonesia. Weakness in investment is not an unprecedented occurrence in IMF-supported programs,[3] but in the Asian crisis countries it appears to have been exacerbated by several factors. Of particular importance

---

[1]Figures here, and below, refer to projections for the fourth reviews of the Korean and Thai programs and the second (Extended Fund Facility) review for Indonesia.

[2]For example, Korea's exports to Japan during the first three quarters of 1998 declined by 20 percent (in U.S. dollar terms) compared with the same period in 1997. Korean exports to other Asian countries contracted similarly, whereas those to the European Union and the United States grew strongly. In Thailand, a broadly similar pattern of export developments was observed in the first half of 1998.

[3]See Goldsbrough and others, 1996.

Figure 5.1. Indonesia, Korea, and Thailand: Domestic and External Demand
(Annual contribution to GDP growth, in percent)

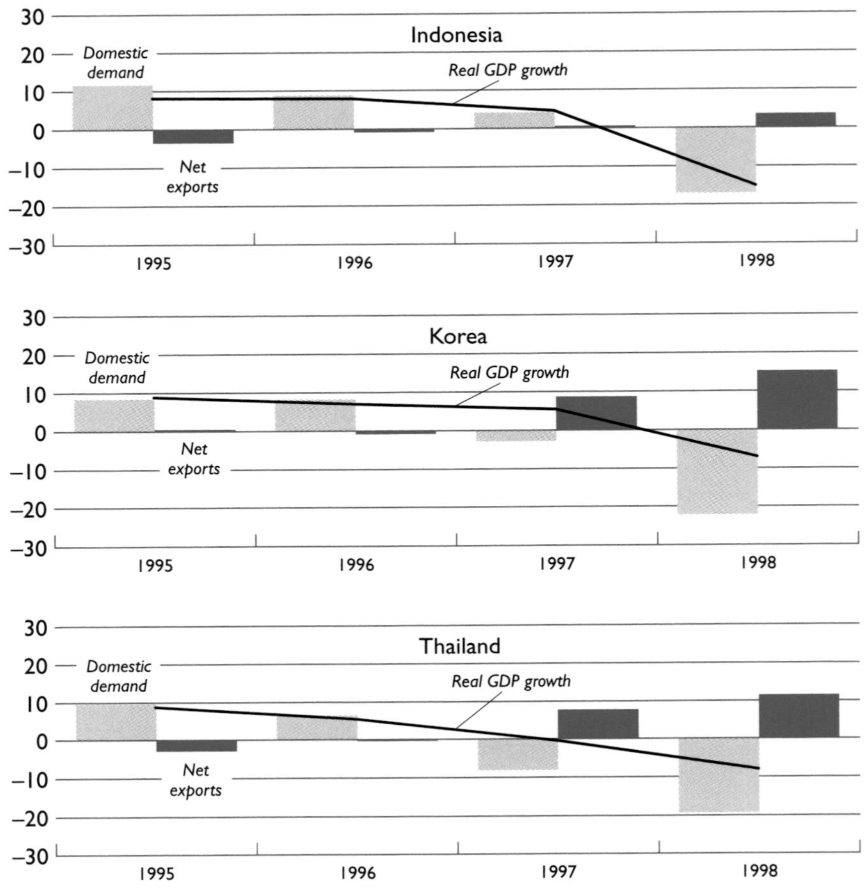

Source: International Monetary Fund, World Economic Outlook.

was the effect of exchange rate depreciations on balance sheets with large unhedged foreign currency liabilities. In addition, investment was battered by the reversal of foreign financing flows and widening of risk premiums, as well as preexisting financial sector weaknesses and the collapse of asset prices. Many corporations (particularly in Korea) were also burdened by excess capacity built up during the preceding investment boom and were in weak financial circumstances (especially as it was nearly impossible for lenders to discriminate between reversible cyclical difficulties and fundamental problems). Moreover, banks facing mounting bad loan problems and low capital-asset ratios were ill-placed to lend. The impact of monetary

policy, another factor affecting investment, will be assessed in the next section.[4]

Private consumption also fell substantially in all three countries: in Korea and Thailand, it fell much more than current income. The rise in savings rates partly reflected wealth effects (corresponding to the balance sheet effects discussed in the previous paragraph) as well as declining confidence. In Indonesia, however, the drop in private consumption

---

[4]Changes in stock building were another important factor in the countries, although measurement problems impede their interpretation. In Korea, in particular, a sharp drop in inventories, largely associated with exports of existing stocks, accounted for a significant portion of export growth in the first half of 1998.

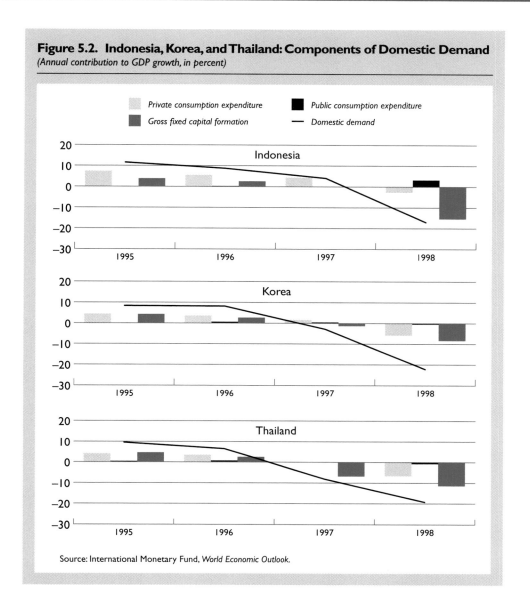

Figure 5.2. Indonesia, Korea, and Thailand: Components of Domestic Demand
(Annual contribution to GDP growth, in percent)

Source: International Monetary Fund, *World Economic Outlook*.

was more or less in line with the (large) decline in income. The behavior of consumption, contrasting with the usual tendency toward consumption smoothing that would lead one to expect a less-than-proportional decline in consumption as output declines, may reflect a combination of liquidity constraints, precautionary saving in the face of increased uncertainty, and expectations of a prolonged slump.

Government consumption made a significant positive contribution to growth in Indonesia, whereas in Korea and Thailand, its contribution was very slightly negative. The impact of fiscal policy on economic activity will be addressed in Section VII below, but at this point it is worth noting that cuts in government consumption were not an important factor contributing to the recession.

Export volumes increased substantially, although values in U.S. dollar terms were reduced by the lowering of dollar export prices. The growth of export volumes was dampened by further shocks to external demand, notably associated with the slowing of economic activity in Japan. Import volumes also declined sharply, as did their value in U.S. dollar terms. The result was that the external sector provided some net support for economic activity in all three countries (Figure 5.3), and the external current accounts underwent major adjustments.

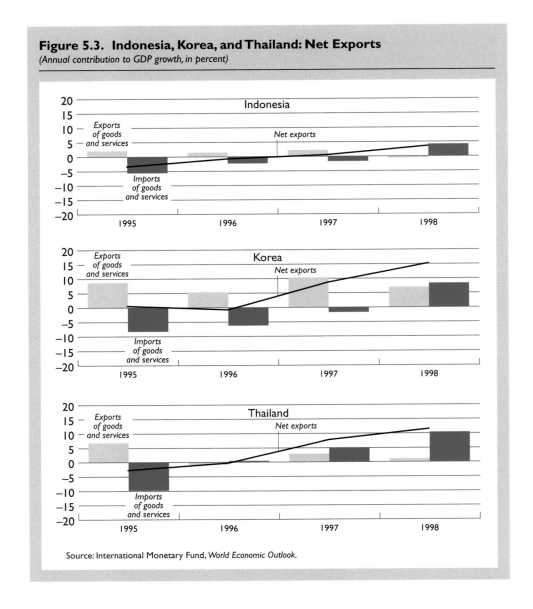

Figure 5.3. Indonesia, Korea, and Thailand: Net Exports
(Annual contribution to GDP growth, in percent)

Source: International Monetary Fund, *World Economic Outlook.*

Supply shocks may also have played a role in the output decline. Aggregate supply may have decreased, in particular, owing to the disruption to production associated with widespread bankruptcies and shifts in the allocation of credit. Moreover, in all three countries, capital has been destroyed by the widespread bankruptcies and large relative price changes associated with crisis, commercial relationships fractured, and "trust" undermined. In Indonesia, civil unrest together with the drought and forest fires likely had a significant negative impact on aggregate supply. However, the fact that export volumes did increase substantially in all three countries suggests that demand-side factors may have played the dominant role in the output decline.

Program Projections

The depth of the slowdown was not foreseen in the initial program projections, and growth projections in particular were revised sharply and successively downward during the course of the programs (Figure 5.4). At the same time, improvements in external current accounts were larger and more rapid than had initially been projected (Figure 5.5). Why were the initial projections so far off the mark?

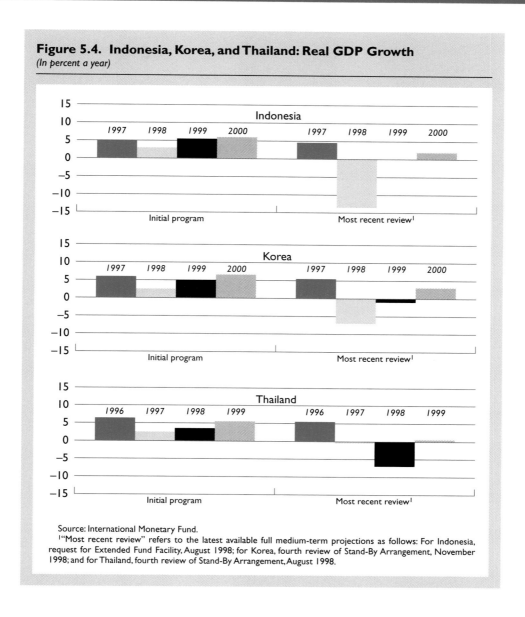

Figure 5.4. Indonesia, Korea, and Thailand: Real GDP Growth
(In percent a year)

Source: International Monetary Fund.
[1]"Most recent review" refers to the latest available full medium-term projections as follows: For Indonesia, request for Extended Fund Facility, August 1998; for Korea, fourth review of Stand-By Arrangement, November 1998; and for Thailand, fourth review of Stand-By Arrangement, August 1998.

First, the program projections for growth were somewhat more optimistic than the consensus at the time. A comparison of program and consensus forecasts[5] shown in Figure 5.6 indicates that the IMF's projections somewhat lagged the consensus in recognizing the severity of the downturn, although they did not differ systematically by large amounts. The fact that the IMF's projections were close to the consensus is not very reassuring, how-ever, as the IMF should in principle have been able to anticipate events better than outside observers. To some extent, optimistic projections appear to have reflected the need to agree with the authorities on a common set of growth assumptions together with the desire to avoid undermining confidence further. However, this may have been counterpro-ductive as the failure of the optimistic projections to be realized may itself have undermined confi-dence in the program.

It is also important to note that program projec-tions are not intended to be unconditional forecasts of economic events. Rather, they are predicated on the successful implementation of the program. The

---

[5]*Consensus Forecasts* publishes projections for GDP growth and other macroeconomic variables of about a dozen institutions. It appears around the middle of each month.

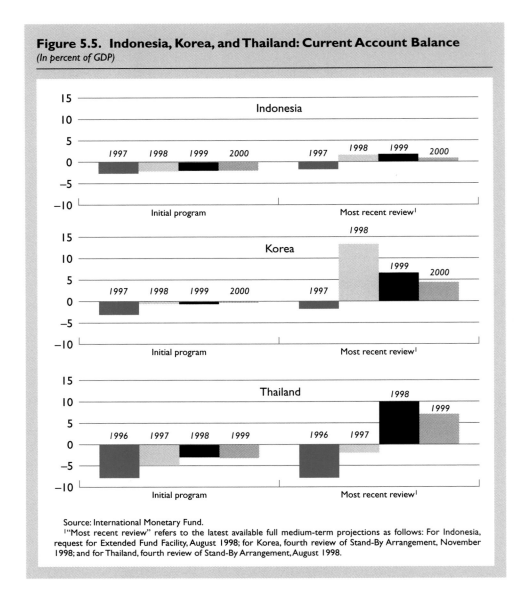

Figure 5.5. Indonesia, Korea, and Thailand: Current Account Balance
(In percent of GDP)

Source: International Monetary Fund.
[1]"Most recent review" refers to the latest available full medium-term projections as follows: For Indonesia, request for Extended Fund Facility, August 1998; for Korea, fourth review of Stand-By Arrangement, November 1998; and for Thailand, fourth review of Stand-By Arrangement, August 1998.

programs were based on a scenario in which confidence was restored and the adverse consequences for growth were therefore contained—but this was only one possible outcome when the programs were formulated and not the one that materialized.

Another noteworthy feature of the projections is that the projections of both the IMF and outsiders were revised progressively downward by very large amounts: very few economists foresaw how deep the slumps would be. To a large extent, the revisions reflected the fact that the magnitude of private capital outflows and the resulting exchange rate depreciations could be factored into the projections only as the crisis unfolded, partly because

they reflected expectations that were self-fulfilling. Some external shocks, such as the further weakening of the Japanese economy, were also not foreseen in advance.

The impression remains, however, that both the IMF and outsiders erred in some ways that could have been avoided at the time. For one thing, the channels of economic interaction among the countries in the region, including both trade and financial sectors, may not have been adequately taken into account when the programs were formulated. Moreover, the experience of Mexico, where growth declined from 4 percent in 1994 to –6 percent in 1995, might have led one to predict a much

Figure 5.6. Consensus Forecasts and Program Forecasts of Real GDP Growth in 1998
(In percent a year)

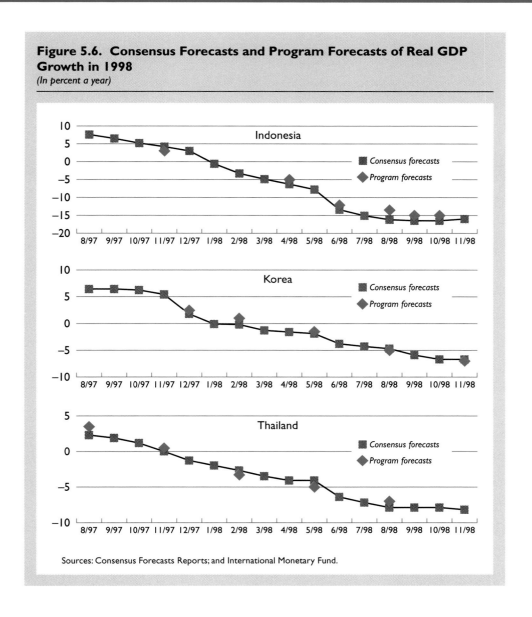

Sources: Consensus Forecasts Reports; and International Monetary Fund.

sharper slowdown in growth than was initially projected in the Asian crisis countries.[6]

Inflation, while it initially exceeded program expectations, at least in Korea and Thailand, turned out

---

[6]The lessons from a wider range of countries are more mixed, however. For example, in a sample of IMF member countries experiencing large exchange rate depreciations of 25 percent or more during 1975–96, the median slowdown in economic growth is only 0.6 percentage point. For countries in this sample whose GDP growth rates prior to the crisis were over 5 percent, the median slowdown is over 4 percentage points—nothing like that which has occurred in the Asian crisis countries.

closer to target than would have been expected given the exchange rate outturns (Figure 5.7). This lower-than-expected pass-through reflects, in part, a decline in import unit values associated with a sharp decline in dollar import prices, and possibly overestimates of the weight of imports in the general price index. Pricing behavior may have reflected weak demand and firms' perceptions that the exchange rate depreciations were temporary. Labor market reactions in the face of growing output gaps were also particularly conducive to price stability: in Korea, in particular, nominal wages actually declined. By mid-1998, inflation was clearly under control in both Korea and Thailand, while it proved more persistent in Indonesia.

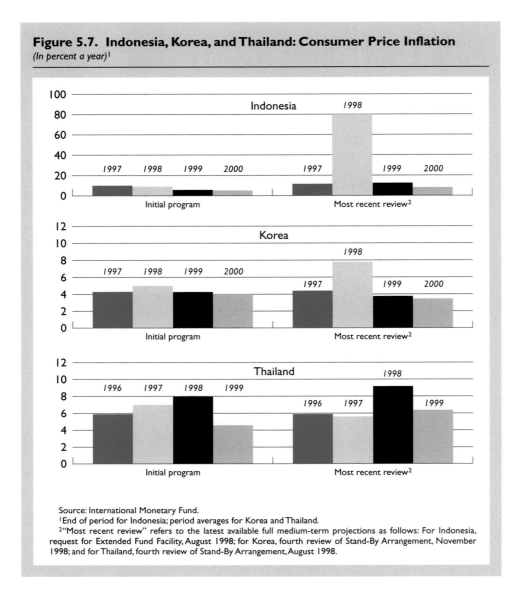

Figure 5.7. Indonesia, Korea, and Thailand: Consumer Price Inflation
(In percent a year)[1]

Source: International Monetary Fund.
[1] End of period for Indonesia; period averages for Korea and Thailand.
[2] "Most recent review" refers to the latest available full medium-term projections as follows: For Indonesia, request for Extended Fund Facility, August 1998; for Korea, fourth review of Stand-By Arrangement, November 1998; and for Thailand, fourth review of Stand-By Arrangement, August 1998.

References

Goldsbrough, David, Sharmini Coorey, Louis Dicks-Mireaux, Balazs Horvath, Kalpana Kochhar, Mauro Mecagni, Erik Offerdal, and Jianping Zhou, 1996, *Reinvigorating Growth in Developing Countries: Lessons from Adjustment Policies in Eight Countries,* IMF Occasional Paper No. 139 (Washington: International Monetary Fund).

International Monetary Fund, 1998, *World Economic Outlook, October 1998: A Survey by the Staff of the International Monetary Fund,* World Economic and Financial Surveys (Washington).

VI Monetary and Exchange Rate Policies

Atish Ghosh and Steven Phillips

Monetary policy in the Asian crisis programs faced a difficult task of balancing two objectives. On the one side was the desire to avoid a depreciation-inflation spiral. During the crisis, exchange rates initially depreciated far beyond real levels consistent with the medium-term fundamentals; had monetary policy fully accommodated these depreciations, the new exchange rates would eventually have been validated by inflation. It could not be taken for granted that these countries' track records of relatively low inflation would be an adequate anchor for market expectations. On the other side were concerns that excessive monetary tightening could severely weaken economic activity.

The programs sought to balance these two concerns. Thus, in the face of the massive portfolio shifts taking place in financial markets, as reflected in substantial increases in country risk premia, policies did not target a preannounced level of the exchange rate, but sought to lean against the wind with a view to averting a depreciation-inflation spiral. While this approach risked following a moving target, a rigid approach was not a practical alternative in the midst of the crisis.

Monetary policy was being carried out in an environment in which high debt-equity ratios in the corporate sectors as well as systemic and structural problems made the financial sector more vulnerable to increases in interest rates. By the same token, these factors, together with the prevalence of unhedged foreign currency liabilities of these countries' financial and corporate sectors, meant that exchange rate depreciation could also have a substantial effect on the real economy.

In Korea and Thailand, policies were eventually tightened as envisaged in the monetary program, preventing the large initial currency depreciations from initiating depreciation-inflation spirals. By the summer of 1998, interest rates had returned to pre-crisis levels and over half of the sharp initial exchange rate depreciation had been reversed. In Indonesia, in contrast, monetary developments were already heading seriously off track by December 1997, reflecting political turbulence and extreme financial system weaknesses. Macroeconomic turmoil ensued, with spiraling inflation, rising risk premiums, continued capital flight, and a dramatic collapse of economic activity. The situation stabilized only in the latter months of 1998.

In Indonesia, monetary policy was emphatically not too tight: on the contrary, nominal interest rates and exchange rates were driven by market risk premiums, while underlying real interest rates remained negative. Money and credit growth accelerated strongly, falling in real terms only subsequently when there were bursts of inflation.

A more difficult question is whether the Thai and Korean programs' successful stabilization caused monetary conditions to become too tight, contributing excessively to the contraction in economic activity. This section examines evidence on various monetary indicators, including interest rates as well as monetary and credit aggregates. By these measures, monetary tightening in these countries was not extreme (in degree or duration) in relation to other crises elsewhere.

At the same time, persistent reports of disruption in access to credit are of concern. Recent and ongoing research examining the possibility of an aggregate credit crunch has not yet generated convincing results—although disruptions in credit markets are a frequent feature of many crisis situations. Moreover, shifts in the distribution of credit, reflecting heightened perceptions of risk, may well have been destabilizing to the activities of specific sectors and enterprises and may at least in part account for perceptions of a credit crunch. To the extent that such microeconomic problems are involved (even if initially triggered by monetary tightening or by the crisis more generally), this would point to the need for progress with corporate and financial restructuring.

Monetary Program Design and Implementation

The behavior of exchange rates through the crisis period varied considerably across the three

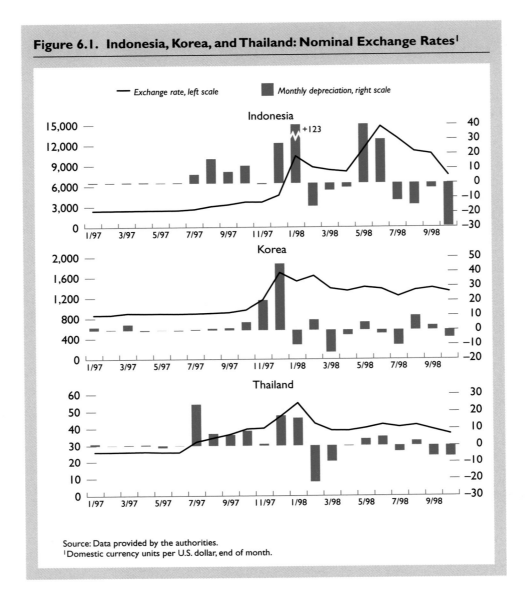

Figure 6.1.   Indonesia, Korea, and Thailand: Nominal Exchange Rates[1]

Source: Data provided by the authorities.
[1]Domestic currency units per U.S. dollar, end of month.

countries (Figure 6.1).[1] In Thailand, after an initial 24 percent depreciation in July 1997, there were a series of smaller (although still substantial) monthly depreciations over a prolonged period, culminating in 16–17 percent depreciations at the end of 1997 and in early 1998, when the rate at last bottomed out. In Korea, substantial depreciation was avoided until late 1997, with the exchange rate

then slipping more abruptly to its weakest point, also in early January 1998. Indonesia's exchange rate, in contrast, depreciated fairly steadily starting in July 1997, with depreciation only reaching above 20 percent a month in December 1997—followed by over 120 percent in January 1998. A limited recovery in the next several months was reversed by large further depreciation in May–June 1998, most of which had been recovered by late October 1998.

Program Design

In pursuing exchange rate stability, the programs made no attempt to stick to a preannounced level or

---

[1]The sharp exchange rate movements make it relatively straightforward to pin down the beginning of the crisis in each country, at least to within a one-month period. For instance, using the definition of a 10 percent depreciation (relative to end-1996) as the beginning of the crisis period gives a starting date of July 1997 for Thailand, August 1997 for Indonesia, and November 1997 for Korea.

range for the exchange rate. Instead, the announced goal was currency stability in the less ambitious sense of avoiding further bouts of rapid depreciation.[2] Programs did assume that varying degrees of nominal appreciation would follow an initial tightening of policy, but these projections were strictly speaking not objectives, since there was no presumption that policy would be tightened by whatever amount necessary to achieve these exchange rate levels.[3]

The strategy strongly emphasized the use of credit and interest rate policies, rather than direct foreign exchange intervention, to restore currency stability. (A notable exception was Indonesia's original program, discussed below.) Some limitation on exchange market intervention was implicit in (end-period) performance criteria on reserves; moreover, informal understandings sought to limit intervention to "smoothing" operations, rather than attempts to counter strong market pressures. The intent was not to preclude resistance to such pressures, but to encourage the use of interest rate policy as the instrument of such resistance as reserves for intervention were in short supply, particularly in Korea and Thailand.

The conduct of monetary policy in the programs was oriented mainly toward interest rates and exchange rates. This approach was appropriate under the circumstances: in particular, given rapidly shifting market conditions, day-to-day policymaking needed to be based on variables that were readily observable. Monetary and credit aggregates were disqualified for this operational role: lags in their measurement limited short-run policy control, and uncertainty about the behavior of money demand in the crisis militated against rigid adherence to preannounced monetary targets. But, at the same time, given market pressures affecting exchange rates and interest rates, and considerable uncertainties over the required real exchange rate adjustment, money and/or credit aggregates, as well as related quantitative variables such as net domestic assets (NDA), were potentially useful indicators that would provide clear-cut warning signals in the event that policy implementation veered substantially off track.

Accordingly, as regards program monitoring, both the Thai and Korean programs used ceilings on NDA of the central bank and floors on net international reserves (NIR) as formal performance criteria. It was presumed that the NDA ceiling would provide an adequate limit on money growth, even though it permitted money to grow faster than programmed in the event—viewed as unlikely—that NIR grew much faster than expected.[4] In addition, as described below, monitoring put a special, less formal, focus on interest rates.

In Indonesia, in contrast, the initial program explicitly provided for "judicious and closely monitored" intervention. This was based on the perception that Indonesia was suffering more from adverse contagion effects and structural weaknesses rather than from traditional macroeconomic imbalances that might require further real depreciation. Accordingly, the performance criterion floor for NIR was set well below the NIR path built into the program's central scenario.[5] In the initial program, this was associated with a ceiling on base money rather than NDA. In principle, adherence to this predetermined base money path should have provided the advantage of a nominal anchor—one consistent with a floating exchange rate regime. However, in a setting with severe market pressures, and in the absence of a policy of clean floating, it turned out to be a weakness: since the NIR floor allowed room for intervention in support of the currency, a base money ceiling would in principle allow most[6] of the monetary impact of any such unprogrammed reserve losses to be sterilized by faster-than-programmed credit expansion, which was an unsustainable and probably ineffective policy response to the severe market pressures.

Since, in all three countries, monetary policy between program reviews was oriented by exchange rates and interest rates, these performance criteria needed to be supplemented by commitments and/or understandings on the behavior of interest rates. Such less formal interest rate understandings, which were set in simple nominal terms, clearly needed to be flexible, to adapt to rapidly changing

---

[2]Over time, as the likelihood of further overwhelming exchange rate pressures seemed to fade, there was a subtle firming of understandings to defend the exchange rate within some band, at least in Thailand.

[3]The Korean program is a case in point. As widely reported in the press, there was an understanding in early 1998 that the authorities would *not reduce* interest rates until the exchange rate had substantially appreciated back to W 1,400 per U.S. dollar. But there was no explicit commitment to *raise* interest rates further if necessary to achieve such appreciation.

[4]This argument, made explicitly in the original Thai program, was based on the assumption of a low probability of a surge in capital inflows. This assumption proved correct, but by 1998 soaring current account surpluses instead created the opportunity for unprogrammed purchases of foreign exchange.

[5]The difference between the floor on NIR and the program's central scenario was not trivial; for the program's first quarterly test date, it was the equivalent of 20 percent of the beginning-of-period base money stock (at program exchange rates).

[6]The program precluded a complete offset; there was a partial adjustor to the base money ceiling to limit such sterilization to four-fifths of any NIR shortfall (while the extent of such intervention would be limited by the NIR floor).

market conditions. There were no specific commitments about how interest rates should be adjusted in *response* to shocks—only understandings defined in broad terms, relying largely on the authorities' good judgment and continuous contact with IMF staff.[7]

In summary, the essential task of monetary policy was to counter the slide of the exchange rate, but there were no specific exchange rate targets. The nominal interest rate—rather than credit or monetary aggregates—was adopted as the de facto gauge and instrument of monetary policy tightening, which together with the exchange rate guided day-to-day policy. This approach has some well-known weaknesses: in particular, an interest rate rule does not provide a nominal anchor. The uncertainties associated with the crisis, however, called for an approach to implementation that emphasized frequent reassessment and flexibility; discretion rather than rules. In this setting, the role of formal performance criteria was generally secondary—that is, they indicated consistency with the central scenario of the program.

Program Implementation

How well did the implementation of monetary policy accord with the programs? From a comparison of actual reserve and broad money developments and their initial program expectations (Figure 6.2),[8] it is immediately obvious that Indonesia's program, approved in November 1997, was already heading seriously off track by the December 1997 test date. Korea and Thailand, however, generally stayed within programmed broad money growth rates, and always well inside expectations for reserve money.[9] Why did Indonesia's program go off track and the others stay on?

The most fundamental problem facing implementation of Indonesia's monetary program was the near-collapse of the banking system during November 1997 through January 1998.[10] Several

banks were insolvent, or at least suffered from serious weaknesses, well before the crisis; the banks' difficulties were compounded by the losses incurred when the rupiah began to depreciate. The closure of some banks, together with the absence of a coherent strategy for dealing with the others (including the scope of guarantees for depositors), was followed by widespread bank runs that led to calls for massive liquidity support from Bank Indonesia. This support, intended to keep the payment system from breaking down, was provided quite indiscriminately, in part because of the difficulties of determining whether individual banks were facing liquidity or solvency problems, fears of contagion, and concern over the drying up of interbank lending reflecting uncertainty about which banks would survive.[11] Such liquidity support, which the central bank made only limited efforts to sterilize, resulted in a massive increase in the NDA of the central bank—which during November 1997 to March 1998 amounted to more than twice the entire stock of base money at the beginning of that period.[12] Although much of the central bank's NDA increase translated into a loss of reserves as Bank Indonesia attempted to arrest the decline of the rupiah, base money was far above its program ceilings, growing by 126 percent (in the six months to March 1998) compared with an original program ceiling of roughly 10 percent.[13] No monetary program could have withstood this kind of stress. As already noted, the design of the original Indonesian program allowed room for unprogrammed intervention to support the currency, to be accompanied by a partially sterilizing increase in NDA; in the event such interventions did occur. Although this was a significant shortcoming in program monitoring, the performance criteria for base money were eventually exceeded (as the excess NDA expansion far outstripped the decline of reserves), signaling clearly that the program was off track. It was thus a flaw in program design, but was by no means the main reason the program went off track. At the time of Indonesia's first program review in April 1998, the monetary program was reformulated in terms of "firm control of NDA of Bank Indonesia," which replaced base money as a performance criterion. The revised program was also intended to dig in heels sharply, by holding both base money and NDA broadly constant through end-1998. How-

---

[7]For instance, understandings might call for nominal rates to be maintained within a certain range for some time, or for cuts in nominal rates to be contingent upon a specified exchange rate outcome. As regards the response to adverse exchange rate shocks, however, program documents tended to state that the authorities understood the need to stand ready to raise interest rates, but were otherwise unspecific.

[8]Figures are for cumulative percent growth, relative to March 1997. The "program expectations" are based on the first program document to specify a projection for that date (usually the initial program document). While there were program revisions, these do not alter the basic story—as discussed below.

[9]Implicit in Figure 6.2, and discussed further below, is the fact that both the Thai and especially the Korean programs *underestimated* the money multiplier.

[10]See also Section VIII below.

[11]During the period between late-1997 and early 1998, for instance, interbank lending may have fallen by as much as two-thirds.

[12]In contrast, in Thailand liquidity support was provided without expanding base money, by recycling reserves from strong to weak banks.

[13]Broad money also grew by an annualized 87 percent during the same period (79 percent excluding foreign currency deposits).

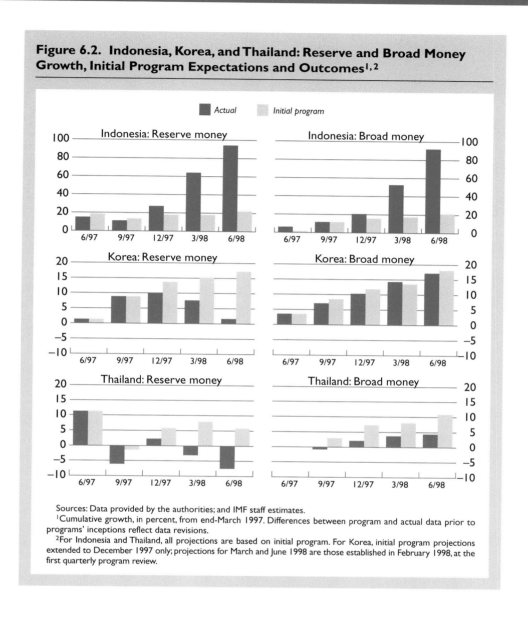

Figure 6.2. Indonesia, Korea, and Thailand: Reserve and Broad Money Growth, Initial Program Expectations and Outcomes[1,2]

Sources: Data provided by the authorities; and IMF staff estimates.
[1]Cumulative growth, in percent, from end-March 1997. Differences between program and actual data prior to programs' inceptions reflect data revisions.
[2]For Indonesia and Thailand, all projections are based on initial program. For Korea, initial program projections extended to December 1997 only; projections for March and June 1998 are those established in February 1998, at the first quarterly program review.

ever, against the background of gathering political unrest, the programmed monetary tightening did not materialize and the program soon went off the new track, with base money and broad money again well above the paths envisaged.[14]

An alternative, more radical solution to monetary policy—a currency board—was also considered by both the IMF staff and the authorities, but ultimately rejected. The continuing banking crisis, the need for legal and institutional changes, and gathering political uncertainty—and serious concerns about continued political interference in monetary policy—argued against this proposal (see Box 6.1).

A new monetary program was established, under calmer conditions, in mid-1998, again envisaging nominal appreciation and calling for base money and NDA to be held broadly flat in the quarter just ahead. As of end-October 1998, monetary developments were essentially on track, and the currency had appreciated dramatically.

[14]The increasing share of foreign currency deposits, which grew to over 30 percent by mid-1998, mainly on account of valuation effects, also seriously complicated control of broad money. Since this share is similar to estimates of the share of imports in the consumer price index (CPI), currency depreciation now automatically generates its own validating increase in liquidity in roughly the same proportion as its direct effect on the price level. Another source of instability is that any withdrawals from foreign currency deposits spilled directly into the foreign exchange market.

Box 6.1. A Currency Board for Indonesia?

A possible alternative method of restoring confidence and stopping the depreciation of a currency is to establish a currency board. Such arrangements have been successfully adopted in a number of IMF-supported stabilization efforts and, soon after the crises broke, serious consideration was given to their possible use, especially in Indonesia.[1] While there are some good arguments in favor, such a regime change was ultimately rejected for Indonesia because of concerns about its credibility and sustainability—especially at an exchange rate far above the prevailing market rate—in the light of ongoing capital outflows as well as practical considerations.

Arguments in favor of a currency board in Indonesia included the following:

- A currency board would end the run on the rupiah. It was felt that the depreciation had entered a "vicious circle" and gone well beyond what was justified on grounds of the changed fundamentals. The strictures of a currency board, and the associated interest rate moves, would reinstill confidence in the domestic currency. While in principle this could also be achieved by a tight-money-based regime, "tying their hands" could allow the authorities to achieve the same credibility faster, with potentially beneficial effects on inflation and growth.[2]

- A currency board would discipline the central bank. In Indonesia, the money supply was chronically difficult to control, given the availability of large central bank liquidity credits to banks and preferred private borrowers. A currency board would facilitate the politically difficult task of severing such credit links.

- A currency board would force a solution to the financial sector problems, by making it clearer which institutions were solvent and circumscribing the central bank's ability to support those that were not. (But this was a two-edged sword, as discussed below.)

There were, however, serious arguments questioning the feasibility of a currency board. Among them:

- If the currency board was less than fully credible— as seemed likely, given turbulent conditions, and market concerns that the authorities may be unable or unwilling to sustain the arrangement—the resulting capital outflow, by automatically contracting the money supply, would lead to punishingly high interest rates.

- In light of the financial sector problems, a currency board—which prevents the central bank from acting as lender of last resort—could only be stable after progress in financial sector reform. In particular, the central bank would either have had to formally revoke deposit guarantees—which would probably have triggered another panic—or committed itself to honoring them—which would not have been feasible in view of available reserves.[3]

- There are legal and institutional requirements for a currency board that are needed to make the system operational.[4] While no specific analysis has been undertaken of what those requirements would be in the case of Indonesia, other countries (with simpler institutional setups) required several months of preparations.

- An unsustainable currency board could have depleted the country's reserves through an exit of capital at a highly appreciated exchange rate, benefiting only those who could get access to the foreign currency before the currency board broke down.

---

[1]Later, the discussion became very public as foreign advisors of the Indonesian government urged the adoption of a currency board.

[2]A study by Ghosh, Gulde, and Wolf (1998) has shown that currency boards have typically had such beneficial effects. That does not, of course, imply that currency boards work equally well in all cases.

[3]See, for example, Santiprabhob (1997).

[4]See Enoch and Gulde (1997).

Indonesia's experience through the first half of 1998 thus emphatically *cannot* be interpreted as reflecting adherence to an overly tight monetary program prescribed by the IMF. The actual outturns bore virtually no relation to program targets. Instead, the main factor driving monetary developments was the hemorrhage of liquidity to a collapsing banking system, which, in the existing political and economic climate, the authorities did little to staunch. A vicious circle developed whereby any policy move toward laxity or accommodation was reflected quickly in currency depreciation, which then further weakened the corporate sector and (hence) banks, leading the central bank to provide even more liquidity support—fueling further depreciation and inflation. Early signals of lack of commitment to the program and later political and social upheavals also contributed to this cycle. It was this climate, and this loss of monetary control, that led Indonesia's nominal interest rates to become the highest in the region, reflecting a widening country risk premium and well-grounded fears of continuing depreciation and inflation.

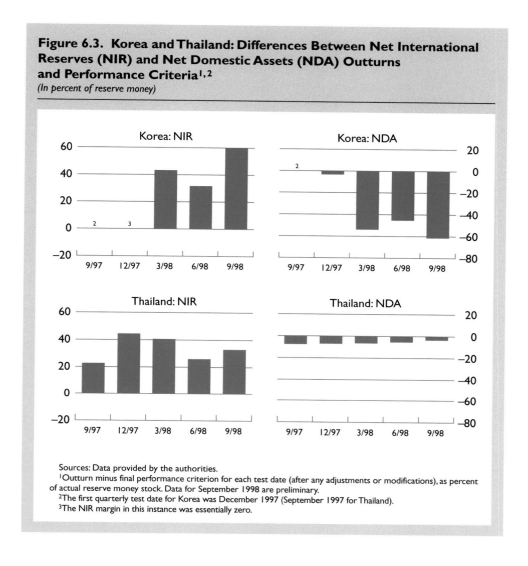

Figure 6.3. Korea and Thailand: Differences Between Net International Reserves (NIR) and Net Domestic Assets (NDA) Outturns and Performance Criteria[1,2]

(In percent of reserve money)

Sources: Data provided by the authorities.
[1]Outturn minus final performance criterion for each test date (after any adjustments or modifications), as percent of actual reserve money stock. Data for September 1998 are preliminary.
[2]The first quarterly test date for Korea was December 1997 (September 1997 for Thailand).
[3]The NIR margin in this instance was essentially zero.

In both Korea and Thailand, in contrast, basic monetary control was maintained. Both reserve and broad money growth rates were generally under, or very close to, original program expectations (see Figure 6.2),[15] and all quarterly NDA and NIR performance criteria through September 1998 were met (Figure 6.3), usually with sizable margins[16]— implying that the programs' formal performance criteria were far from being a binding constraint on the conduct of monetary policy in pursuit of exchange rate stability.[17]

---

[15]It should be noted that not only in Indonesia, but also in Korea and Thailand, banking sector troubles complicated the conduct of monetary policy. For example, in mid-December 1997, still early in Korea's program, the Bank of Korea injected liquidity of about W 8 trillion, or more than one-third of reserve money at end-November 1997. In contrast to the Indonesian case, the authorities quickly sterilized this large injection.

[16]The interpretation of such margins requires some caution, however. For example, rather than tighter-than-programmed central bank credit, the large NDA margins in Korea in fact re-flect NIR developments. In general, accumulation of NIR through means other than exchange market intervention (for example, sovereign bond issues, or the repayment of foreign loans extended by the central bank, in excess of program assumptions) leaves reserve money unchanged, so that measured NDA contracts even with unchanged credit policy. If NDA ceilings are not adjusted downward for such contingencies, large margins can result.

[17]Of course, these margins are also consistent with the interpretation that the de facto interest rate targets were set too high to be consistent with the reserve and broad money growth targets. Hence, it is essential also to examine the behavior of nominal and real interest rates, as is done later in the section.

The path of *nominal* interest rates differed between Korea and Thailand. In Korea, the authorities were initially reluctant to raise interest rates, but did so abruptly in the face of the funding crisis in late December 1997, and thereafter seem to have followed the path one would expect of a successful currency stabilization effort, that is, a very *gradual* decline, reaching precrisis levels by mid-1998. Importantly, Korea avoided the syndrome—earlier found in Indonesia and to a lesser degree in Thailand, in 1997—in which interest rates are eased too soon in the currency stabilization effort, forcing a return to yet higher rates, presumably with a loss of credibility and, hence, effectiveness in the process.

Monetary Policy Stance

The next question is whether the monetary stance in these programs was appropriate—that is, whether the right balance was struck between the twin objectives of exchange rate and output stability. This section addresses this question based on available indicators of monetary policy, as well as with reference to the experience of other countries facing exchange rate crises.

In none of the countries did monetary policy go to the limit needed to ensure absolute exchange rate stability. This is implicit in the decision not to repeg exchange rates at any predetermined level and is also obvious from the fact that the currency depreciations in all three countries went well beyond any reasonable estimate of the real exchange rate adjustment required. However, from a slightly longer perspective, the fact that Korea's and Thailand's currencies recovered substantially by mid-1998 as interest rates declined to precrisis levels and inflation remained subdued suggests that with these policies stability is being restored. (Indonesia's progress on the stabilization came later in the year, following the eventual firming of monetary policy.)

Another indication of the impact of monetary policy in stabilizing the exchange rate is the dollar rates of return expected by investors (that is, domestic rates of return corrected for expected currency depreciation). To provide a disincentive for the exit of capital, expected dollar returns would need at the very least to be positive—and more generally, would be expected to exceed the safe rate on dollar deposits by a margin sufficient to compensate for higher risk. Expected monthly dollar returns (based on surveys of exchange rate forecasts)[18] are estimated to have been negative for

some periods during 1997 in both Korea and Thailand, becoming strongly positive by February 1998 (Figure 6.4).[19] This suggests that interest rates were initially inadequate to offer sufficient incentive to hold those currencies, but became high enough in early 1998. This, together with the large depreciations of the currencies that occurred in late 1997, suggests that policies would have needed to have been tightened sooner to arrest the currency depreciations.[20] There was also a stop-go element to monetary tightening (see Figure 6.5)—with a tendency, especially in Thailand in 1997, to lower nominal interest rates at the first signs of exchange rate stability—which may have contributed to undermining policy credibility and heightening perceptions of exchange rate risk. (To the extent that there is contagion—as discussed in Box 6.2—negative returns in one country might also spark higher risk premiums in others.) In Indonesia, in contrast, dollar rates of return were negative in the early months of the program, then pushed up to high levels in the spring of 1998 with increasing political and social unrest.

A further question is whether the authorities should have pushed interest rates to much higher levels in order to stabilize the exchange rate. In addition to concerns over the likely effects of such a policy on the real economy, it is not clear that this approach would have been successful in stabilizing exchange rates under the conditions prevailing in early 1998. For one thing, real interest rates far higher than those that actually prevailed might have had little favorable impact on international capital flows, or may even have had a perverse effect, owing to their impact on balance sheets that were already crippled by the currency depreciations. Some critics of the monetary programs in the Asian crisis have argued that such perverse effects actually materialized but as yet no convincing evi-

---

[18]See also Goldfajn and Baig (1998).

[19]An analysis of ex post dollar rates of return indicates that realized returns were consistently negative from July 1997 in Thailand and September 1997 in Korea, but turned sharply positive in February 1998.

[20]Another benchmark for policies is the contraction in real money needed to stabilize exchange rates in the face of an increase in risk premiums demanded by investors. IMF staff simulations suggest that, to have stabilized exchange rates in the face of an assumed 10 percentage point shock to the risk premium would have required contractions in the broad money/GDP ratio of 3 percent to 10 percent in 1997 relative to 1996. In contrast, as discussed below, real money balances continued to *grow* in the second half of 1997 in both Indonesia and Korea, although in Thailand they did decline in 1997 (by about 5 percent). A tightening of monetary conditions (as measured by real money balances) in Korea and Thailand starting in January 1998 was associated with greater nominal exchange rate stability. Real money also declined in Indonesia in the first quarter of 1998, but this was more a reflection of mounting inflation than of policy tightening.

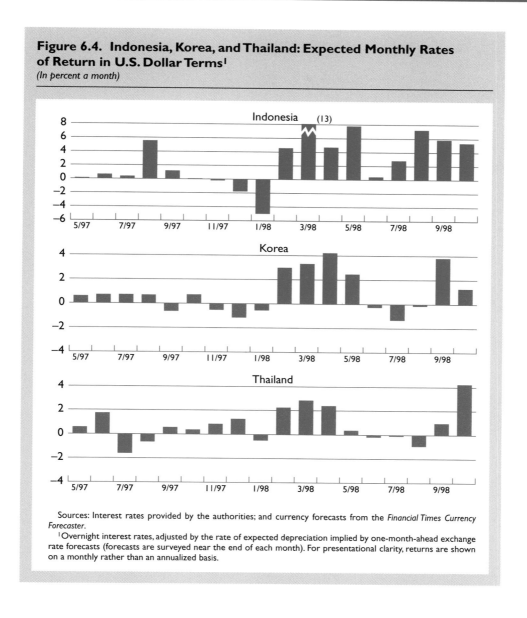

Figure 6.4. Indonesia, Korea, and Thailand: Expected Monthly Rates of Return in U.S. Dollar Terms[1]
(In percent a month)

Sources: Interest rates provided by the authorities; and currency forecasts from the *Financial Times Currency Forecaster*.

[1]Overnight interest rates, adjusted by the rate of expected depreciation implied by one-month-ahead exchange rate forecasts (forecasts are surveyed near the end of each month). For presentational clarity, returns are shown on a monthly rather than an annualized basis.

dence has been presented showing that interest rates reached levels at which such perverse effects would be important (Box 6.3).

Another issue is the transmission mechanism: in at least some of these countries, the range of short-term domestic currency financial instruments is limited,[21] narrowing the scope for higher interest rates to lure investors into domestic currency assets. Notwithstanding the latter observation, however,

there were still important channels through which domestic interest rates could influence capital flows and the exchange rate: exporters faced a trade-off between holding foreign assets and repatriating revenues; banks could intermediate capital flows in the form of deposits or direct borrowing from the capital markets; and residents faced a trade-off between holding domestic and foreign deposits (although these mechanisms were no doubt impaired by the sorry—and worsening—state of domestic banking systems).

Another indicator that is particularly relevant with regard to the implications of monetary policy for real activity is the behavior of real interest rates, as shown in Figure 6.5. In Indonesia, real

---

[21]Notably, in Indonesia the Balanced Budget Law prohibits domestic financing of a government deficit, which has contributed to stifling the development of a domestic government bond market. See, for example, Molho (1994).

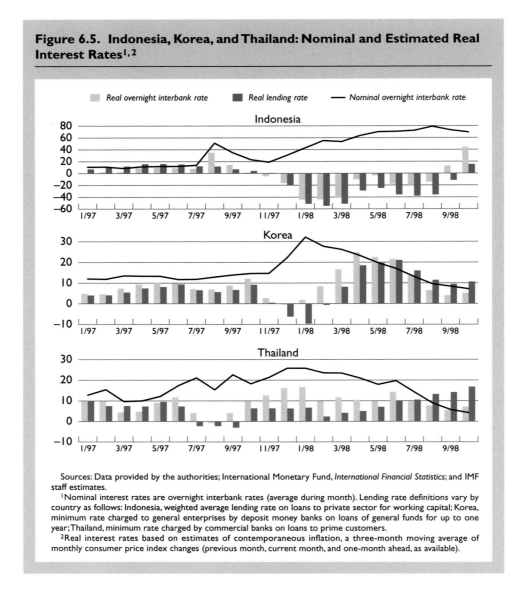

Figure 6.5. Indonesia, Korea, and Thailand: Nominal and Estimated Real Interest Rates[1,2]

Real overnight interbank rate   Real lending rate   —— Nominal overnight interbank rate

Sources: Data provided by the authorities; International Monetary Fund, *International Financial Statistics*; and IMF staff estimates.
[1]Nominal interest rates are overnight interbank rates (average during month). Lending rate definitions vary by country as follows: Indonesia, weighted average lending rate on loans to private sector for working capital; Korea, minimum rate charged to general enterprises by deposit money banks on loans of general funds for up to one year; Thailand, minimum rate charged by commercial banks on loans to prime customers.
[2]Real interest rates based on estimates of contemporaneous inflation, a three-month moving average of monthly consumer price index changes (previous month, current month, and one-month ahead, as available).

overnight and lending rates were consistently negative from late 1997 through August 1998. In contrast, in Korea and Thailand, real rates became very low or negative in the months immediately following the onset of the exchange rate crisis, but since then they have been consistently positive.[22] In

_____

[22]Figure 6.5 shows the evolution of two real interest rate measures—the overnight and average lending rate, deflated by an estimate of contemporaneous CPI inflation. Whereas the CPI represents the real interest rate relevant to household, the wholesale price index (WPI) may be a better indicator of the real interest burden on manufacturers; the WPI increased more rapidly than the CPI in these countries, so the CPI-deflated interest rate if anything overstates the real interest burden. The lending rate shown is taken from the *International Financial*

Thailand, real interest rates rose to an average 13 percent in the fourth quarter of 1997 and the first quarter of 1998, falling to 11 percent in the second quarter of 1998, and then declined further. In Korea, nominal rates were raised sharply in late 1997, and after a strong but brief surge of inflation, real rates became quite high by historical standards, averaging more than 20 percent in the second quarter of 1998; Korea's nominal interest rates have declined quite steadily since their January 1998 peak, and by August 1998 were back to near

_____

Statistics, and is not fully comparable across countries. (See Figure 6.5 for details.)

Box 6.2. High-Frequency Contagion in the Exchange and Equity Markets

One of the factors complicating stabilization efforts during the East Asian crisis was the contagion across countries. Such contagion effects arise because of trade and financial linkages, or because events in one country change perceptions about prospects in others, or simply because of herd behavior on the part of investors.

While there are various measures of contagion, perhaps the simplest and most robust is the correlation of exchange rate (or stock market price) movements across countries. These correlations rose significantly in the latter half of 1997 and, while falling somewhat more recently, remain positive and significant. Using a sample consisting of Indonesia, Korea, Malaysia, the Philippines, and Thailand, the accompanying table reports a panel regression of daily exchange rate (or stock market price) movement in one country on the average exchange rate (stock market price) movement in the four *other* countries (denoted the "contagion" variable).[1]

According to the estimates, a 1 percent average depreciation in the four other countries is associated with a 0.38 percent depreciation in the country's own exchange rate.[2] Indeed, there is Granger causality from the contagion

variable to changes in the country's own exchange rate—that is, the contagion variable helps predict movements in that country's exchange rate even when past movements in the same country's exchange rate are taken into account. A 1 percent contagion depreciation is associated with a 0.31 depreciation on the following day, controlling for lagged changes in the country's own exchange rate.

More recently, the contagion effect has diminished in magnitude, while remaining positive and highly statistically significant. Finally, it is worth noting that contagion effects are discernible not only at very high frequencies but also with monthly data, and are robust to the inclusion of the country's interest rate (either in levels or in first differences).

The results for stock market prices are broadly similar. Estimating the regression over the period July 1997 to June 1998 shows that a 1 percent decline in the average stock prices of the four other countries is associated with a 0.64 percent decline in the country's own stock price. There is, however, some evidence of this "contagion" effect as far back as 1996 (albeit of smaller magnitude). As with exchange rate movements, the contagion variable Granger causes subsequent movements in stock market prices.

---

[1]Also included in the regression, but not reported, are four lags of the dependent variable and the dollar-yen exchange rate.

[2]It is also noteworthy that the significance of the contagion variable increases in the crisis period (interacting the contagion variable with a dummy variable for the period July

1997–May 1998 yields a coefficient of 0.76, *t*-statistic 3.56**), although this may also reflect the greater flexibility of exchange rates in the crisis period than before.

Contagion in Exchange and Equity Markets

	Exchange Rate, $\Delta\log(e)$		Stock Market Price, $\Delta\log(p)$	
	Daily	Monthly	Daily	Monthly
Contemporaneous contagion, Jan.–Dec. 1996				
Coefficient	−0.016	−0.308	0.443	0.473
t-statistic	−0.22	−1.12	7.33	2.28
R^2	0.02	0.20	0.11	0.17
Contemporaneous contagion, July 1997–June 1998				
Coefficient	0.380	0.604	0.643	0.831
t-statistic	5.64	3.80	12.96	4.94
R^2	0.10	0.23	0.23	0.45
Lagged contagion (Granger causality), July 1997–June 1998				
Coefficient	0.314	−0.007	0.235	0.412
t-statistic	3.53	−0.02	3.97	1.49
R^2	0.07	0.08	0.05	0.11
Contemporaneous contagion, Jan.–May 1998				
Coefficient	0.359	0.503	0.763	0.915
t-statistic	4.34	2.61	12.12	2.78
R^2	0.12	0.24	0.32	0.43
Lagged contagion (Granger causality), Jan.–May 1998				
Coefficient	0.349	0.067	0.288	1.434
t-statistic	2.74	0.18	3.22	4.46
R^2	0.08	0.16	0.05	0.58

Source: IMF staff estimates.

Box 6.3. Episodic Evidence on the Interest Rate-Exchange Rate Relationship

A number of recent studies have tried to assess empirically whether higher interest rates are useful in supporting the exchange rate (that is, the "traditional" effect) or whether they instead have an opposite, "perverse" effect. Rather than examining the long-run relationship between monetary policy and the exchange rate, these studies focus on patterns inside selected short episodes.

The results of these studies are inconclusive and indeed quite mixed. In general, they fail to find overwhelming evidence of the traditional effect—though this is not surprising, given the inherent policy endogeneity problem (that is, interest rates are likely to be raised precisely during episodes of currency depreciation, as both variables respond to shifts in market sentiment). On the other hand, neither is there a clear pattern of evidence across studies of a perverse effect of interest rate policy.

Furman and Stiglitz (1998) identify a set of 13 episodes, in nine emerging markets, of "temporarily high" interest rates (episodes in which interest rates rose by more than 10 percentage points for at least five days, then fell back). Using a simple regression analysis, they find that both the magnitude and duration of such interest rate hikes are associated with exchange rate *depreciation*. While Furman and Stiglitz note that this evidence is not definitive, and that its interpretation is fraught with difficulties concerning endogeneity, they conclude that it at least questions the usefulness of raising interest rates.

Kraay (1998) focuses instead on episodes of speculative attacks on currencies and uses a more sophisticated and complex methodology. He identifies a set of 121 attacks that were successful, in the sense that there was an uncharacteristically large monthly depreciation; he also identifies (with greater inherent difficulty) a set of 192 unsuccessful attacks. The essential finding is that increases in central bank discount rates are neither necessary nor sufficient for staving off a speculative attack. Indeed, no relationship is found between central bank discount policy and the success or failure of speculative attacks. When Kraay tries to control for the endogeneity of interest rate policy, the results are similar, although,

as he notes, they are preliminary and could reflect the difficulty of specifying appropriate instrumental variables to control for policy endogeneity.

Goldfajn and Gupta (1998) ask a somewhat different question, one probably more relevant for the East Asian countries during their IMF-supported programs. They consider cases *following* an exchange rate crisis in which the real exchange rate has become clearly undervalued, so that considerable real appreciation is likely to follow. They then study whether tighter monetary policies—in terms of higher-than-average real interest rates—are associated with the corrective real appreciation occurring mainly through currency appreciation rather than through higher inflation.

In general, Goldfajn and Gupta find that tight monetary policy does raise the probability of "success"; that is, achieving the corrective real appreciation via currency appreciation. However, when the sample is restricted to cases where the banking sector is fragile, tight monetary policy seems to reduce the probability of success (though as the authors note, this latter result is based on very few cases and is not robust).

Goldfajn and Baig (1998), rather than defining and identifying crisis episodes from a broad sample of countries, focus on the very recent experience of five Asian countries, from mid-1997 through May 1998. Using daily data, they analyze the relationship between nominal interest rates and nominal exchange rates during the recent Asian crisis. A vector autoregression does not find a significant relationship—in either direction—for any of the five Asian countries. On the other hand, a panel regression using *changes* in interest rates and exchange rates yields a traditionally signed coefficient over all the sample spans examined, though this is statistically significant only in some subperiods. Country-by-country regressions find a significant traditionally signed coefficient in some periods for Indonesia, Korea, and the Philippines (the only significant coefficient with the opposite sign is found for Malaysia, and this in one subperiod only). Goldfajn and Baig thus conclude that their study finds no evidence that higher interest rates lead to weaker exchange rates; if anything, there are periods where higher rates lead to stronger exchange rates.

---

precrisis levels.[23] In sum, it is far from clear that the path of real interest rates has implied a sustained or crushing burden on economic activity. Moreover, the initial increases in real interest rates

were certainly less aggressive than those seen occasionally in other countries during exchange rate crises or in their immediate aftermath, as discussed in Box 6.4.

Real interest rates may not provide an adequate measure of the tightness of monetary conditions if the *volumes* of liquidity and/or lending are falling sharply in nominal or real terms. Real broad money, in Indonesia and Korea, however, far from severely contracting, continued growing in the second half of 1997 and the first half of 1998—albeit

---

[23]Appendix 6.1 reports ex ante real interest rates, based on a simple inflation forecasting model that relates CPI inflation to its own lag, and lagged changes in broad money and the exchange rate. The implied ex ante real interest rates are somewhat lower for Korea and Thailand, because actual inflation has been "unexpectedly" low (even in relation to the historically low exchange rate pass-through coefficients).

Box 6.4. High Interest Rates in International Perspective

Although interest rates in East Asia rose in early 1998, they typically fell shy of the very high nominal and real interest rates occasionally seen in some other countries during (or in the aftermath of) an exchange rate crisis.

In *Sweden*, the Riksbank raised its marginal lending rate to 75 percent a year on September 8, 1992 in defense of the krona's parity in the exchange rate mechanism. Interest rates were lowered the following week, but on September 16, renewed turmoil in the currency markets forced an increase in the marginal lending rate, first to 75 percent a year, and later that afternoon, to an unprecedented 500 percent a year. Effective September 21, the marginal lending rate was lowered to 50 percent a year, and, in early October, to 20 percent. Through October and early November, the marginal rate was decreased by degrees to 11.5 percent. During the crisis, interbank interest rates averaged 82 percent in September 1992 (74 percent in real terms), falling to 17 percent in October 1992, and remaining above 10 percent until March 1993. During the four-day period of 500 percent interest rates, however, banks were protected by loans on more favorable terms.

In *Mexico*, following the sharp devaluation of the peso in December 1994, there were sharp increases in nominal interest rates, with the average cost of funds for banks rising from 17 percent a year to almost 60 percent a year in the first quarter of 1995. Set against inflation of over 70 percent (at annual rates), however, real interest rates were not especially high. Nominal interest rates then dipped to 35 percent in the third quarter, before ending the year at about 47 percent. Thereafter, interest rates fell steadily, to 40 percent by the end of the first quarter of 1996, and 20 percent by the first quarter of 1997. Other interest rates in the economy followed a similar pattern, with the nominal interest rate on commercial paper peaking at 112 percent a year (in the first quarter of 1995), dipping to 47 percent a year in the third quarter of 1995, and ending the year at 70 percent. By the first quarter of 1997, the nominal rate on commercial paper had fallen to 30 percent a year.

Deflated by the consumer price index, the real rate on commercial paper actually fell in the first quarter of 1995 (from 11 percent a year to 6.5 percent a year) before increasing to 15 percent a year at end-1995, and 22 percent a year in the first quarter of 1996. Since then, real interest rates have fallen steadily.

In *Argentina*, the aftermath of the Mexican crisis triggered a capital outflow in early 1995, with deposits in the Argentine banking system declining by some $8 billion, and interbank and deposit rates rising to about 20–30 percent a year in March 1995 (against an annual inflation rate of below 2 percent). A series of measures, including a substantial fiscal adjustment package, helped restore confidence, and by July 1995, lending rates had fallen to 15 percent a year, and by April 1996, they were 10 percent a year.

In the *Czech Republic* interest rates were raised briefly—with overnight interbank rates reaching 60 percent in nominal terms (against an annual inflation rate of 10 percent)—during the exchange rate crisis in May 1997. The authorities decided to abandon the exchange rate band and adopted a managed float instead. Following the crisis, interbank interest rates fell quickly, and within three months were at 14½ percent (about 2 percentage points above the precrisis level).

In the *Slovak Republic*, one-month interbank interest rates rose to 25–26 percent (against an annual inflation rate of 6 percent) in May 1997, following a speculative attack on the koruna.

---

at slower rates than previously (Figure 6.6).[24] In Thailand, real money did contract steadily, but not dramatically, by about 5 percent from mid-1997 through mid-1998.

There was also little evidence of tightening real credit during the second half of 1997. The measured stock of credit grew in real terms at annualized rates ranging from 13 percent in Korea, to 15 percent in Thailand, to almost 40 percent in Indonesia.[25]

Credit growth decelerated in all three countries in the first half of 1998: in Indonesia, there was only a slight deceleration of a rapid growth rate (to an annualized 32 percent), while in Korea real credit declined by an annualized 3 percent and in Thailand by 11 percent.

The slowing of growth rates of money and credit, although not inconsequential, appears to be far from draconian. Despite dire warnings that tightening monetary policies in the midst of a banking crisis would lead to a financial implosion, nothing

---

[24]For Korea, where inflation has been minimal and household saving has been increasing, the growth of real balances may reflect an increase in money demand. In Indonesia, however, it is more likely related to lags in the money-inflation relationship.

[25]One caveat regarding the interpretation of these measured changes is that some of the increased credit reflected valuation changes affecting foreign-currency-denominated credit—a factor that was particularly important in Indonesia. The measure presented includes these valuation changes (consistent with the treatment of the effects of inflation) as they nonetheless affect the amount of real financing or real liquidity being provided to the economy. An alternative approach, based on credit flows, gives a different month-to-month pattern but does not greatly alter the overall picture.

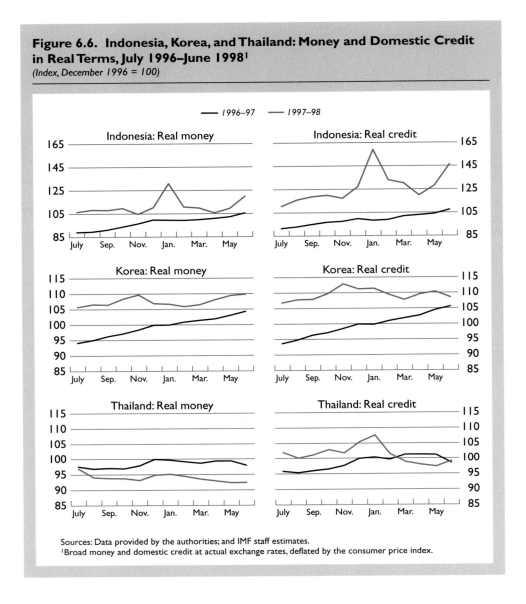

Figure 6.6. Indonesia, Korea, and Thailand: Money and Domestic Credit in Real Terms, July 1996–June 1998[1]
(Index, December 1996 = 100)

Sources: Data provided by the authorities; and IMF staff estimates.
[1]Broad money and domestic credit at actual exchange rates, deflated by the consumer price index.

like that has occurred.[26] It is useful to compare them with the degree of tightening found in the experience of other countries facing exchange rate crises. Table 6.1 reports the money and credit developments surrounding three such episodes—the Czech Republic in May 1997, Mexico in December 1994, and Sweden in November 1992. In the year of an episode of substantial depreciation, not only did real money and credit growth tend to slow compared with the previous year, there were generally real *contractions* of money and credit. In the Asian countries, in contrast—though there have been lower rates of growth of real money and credit—only in Thailand have actual (real) contractions occurred. With regard to the deceleration of real money growth, Mexico stands out: although money growth accelerated in nominal terms, it was greatly outpaced by a surge in inflation that lowered the growth of real money by almost 26 percentage points between 1994 and 1995—while the growth rate of real GDP declined by almost 10 percentage points. The slowdown in real money and credit in the Asian programs pales in comparison.

What impact did this monetary tightening have on the economies of the Asian crisis countries? Some il-

---

[26]In the classic example of the United States during the Great Depression, the nominal money stock fell by one-third (Lebergott, 1984).

Table 6.1. Czech Republic, Mexico, and Sweden: Money and Credit Developments Surrounding Episodes of Devaluation or Depreciation

	Czech Republic	Mexico	Sweden
	(Twelve-month rates of change, in percent)[1]		
Broad money			
Year t[2]	7.9	33.3	4.4
Year $t-1$	9.2	21.7	3.0
Year $t-2$	19.8	14.5	4.5
Domestic credit			
Year t[2]	10.1	22.8	2.9
Year $t-1$	10.8	31.5	−12.8
Year $t-2$	13.7	12.7	−0.1
Real money			
Year t[2]	−1.9	−12.3	0.4
Year $t-1$	0.6	13.6	1.2
Year $t-2$	11.0	6.0	−3.2
Real domestic credit			
Year t[2]	0.1	−19.2	−1.1
Year $t-1$	2.0	22.8	−14.3
Year $t-2$	5.4	4.4	−7.4
Memorandum items:			
CPI inflation (end of period)			
Year t[2]	10.0	52.0	4.0
Year $t-1$	8.6	7.1	1.8
Year $t-2$	7.9	8.0	7.9
Currency depreciation[3]			
Year t[2]	27.0	95.0	21.6
Year $t-1$	2.6	26.5[4]	19.3
Year $t-2$	−5.5	−0.3	2.8
Real GDP growth			
Year t[2]	1.5	−6.1	−2.2
Year $t-1$	4.1	4.4	−1.4
Year $t-2$	5.9	2.0	−1.7

[1]GDP figures are year-on-year.

[2]"Year t" refers to 1997 for the Czech Republic, 1995 for Mexico, and 1993 for Sweden. Abrupt depreciations took place in 1997 in the Czech Republic, in late 1994 in Mexico, and in late 1992 in Sweden.

[3]Measured as the change in the number of domestic currency units per U.S. dollar.

[4]Reflects devaluation in late 1994 (through November 1994, the 12-month depreciation was only 9.1 percent).

lustrative calculations are presented in Appendix 6.1, based on estimated impulse response functions of real GDP growth to a given deceleration of the growth of real money. These calculations suggest that for Korea and Thailand, the estimated effects of monetary tightening could account for less than one-fourth of the expected negative swing in GDP growth rates from 1997 to 1998, and a very small part of the deceleration expected for Indonesia. However, the actual effects could be even smaller, since the technique used attributes all money-growth correlation to money's influence on growth. (On the other hand, the historical relationships examined are unlikely to capture the banking-related sensitivity of output.)

Thus, available monetary indicators tend to contradict the view that monetary policy was tightened drastically in these countries and that this tightening was a major reason for the economic slowdown in the Asian crisis countries. Indeed, events in Indonesia display a breakdown of monetary control rather than severe tightening. How can this evidence be reconciled with widespread perceptions of a continuing "credit crunch" in these countries? Clearly, what the aggregate data cannot capture is a shift in credit allocation among different borrowers, in the face of widespread bankruptcies and an increased preoccupation of financial institutions with credit risk (associated in part with the tightening of prudential regulations). It would not be surprising if, in this environment, many borrowers that previously had access to credit (especially small and medium-sized enterprises) found themselves unable to obtain financing. The counterpart of this cutoff of access to credit could be an increased share of credit going to capitalize interest on loans to companies perceived as more creditworthy (especially to larger companies, as is reported to be the case in Korea). The possibility of a credit crunch in these countries is still being studied, and some preliminary evidence is discussed in Box 6.5. Disruptions in credit markets are clearly of concern although not uncommon in such circumstances.[27] To the extent that they reflect structural problems in credit allocation, the main solution is to move ahead with the needed restructuring of financial systems and workout of corporate debt (as discussed in Section VIII below).

Conclusion

Monetary policy, albeit only after some period, achieved its basic objective of avoiding a depreciation/inflation spiral in both Korea and Thailand—without necessitating persistently and egregiously high real interest rates, and without causing a collapse of nominal, or even real, money or credit volumes. This is not to deny, of course, that monetary tightening had a cost for the real economy, but the alternative would have been more costly.

The currency crisis might have been less severe had stabilization been pursued earlier, more aggressively, and more consistently. In the early part of 1998, in contrast, there was some tightening of monetary conditions in Korea and Thailand—accompanied by greater signs of exchange rate stability (and even nominal appreciation). Going much further in the direction of tightening at this late stage, however, might have proved counterproductive, given the effects of much higher interest rates on balance sheets of banks and corporations already reeling from the effects of the currency depreciations.

The pattern of real interest rates in Korea and Thailand is not untypical of stabilization episodes: initially low or negative real rates as inflation surges, followed by a period of high real interest rates as nominal rates lag declining inflation. The authorities' reaction to this second phase is critical: either the impact of high interest rates on the real economy leads them to abandon the stabilization

effort—confirming the doubts that were reflected in market pressures on interest rates—or they persevere and are able gradually to lower nominal and real interest rates as reforms succeed and gain credibility. It is precisely the first possibility that undermines confidence and makes the deft handling of interest rate policy crucial. During this process, some period of high real interest rates is probably unavoidable. The challenge is to ease rates down without jeopardizing stabilization. Ultimately, the decline in nominal and real interest rates needs to come more from smaller risk premiums and greater confidence, rather than from expanding money and credit.

Monetary policy in Indonesia, until the stabilization of recent months, is quite a different story: a virtually complete loss of monetary control in the face of the banking collapse and political turmoil, resulting in high nominal interest rates that reflected risk premiums while real interest rates remained negative. The resulting, highly expansionary, monetary policy was reflected in a lurch into high inflation, capital outflows, and a collapse of the currency. This experience illustrates the danger that even in a previously stable economy, a vicious circle of inflation and depreciation can emerge.

Appendix 6.1. Monetary and Exchange Rate Policies

Earlier in this section, reference was made to various results. This appendix provides details of the calculations on the following:

- the monetary contraction required to offset a given increase in the risk premium;

- the expected real interest rate; and

- the impact of a given monetary contraction on real GDP growth.

Monetary Contraction Required to Offset a Given Increase in the Risk Premium

This section raised the question what magnitude of monetary contraction would have stabilized the exchange rate, given an exogenous increase in the risk premium demanded by investors. This requires an explicit model of the exchange rate. The simplest such framework is the monetary model of exchange rate determination. In such a model, real demand for broad money depends positively on the level of activity and negatively on the interest rate. Domestic and foreign interest rates are linked by a

---

[27]Moreover, credit crunches have sometimes occurred in the absence of either a currency crisis or severe monetary policy tightening, for example, in the United States in 1990–91.

Box 6.5. Was There a Credit Crunch?

In recent months, there has been much discussion about a "credit crunch" in the East Asian economies—most notably in Indonesia, Korea, and Thailand. While there was clearly a sharp fall in external finance available, the debate has centered on whether domestic credit conditions tightened significantly, and perhaps excessively.

The term credit crunch is perhaps best understood as a situation in which, *at prevailing interest rates*, there is an unsatisfied excess demand for credit. In the present context, however, the term has been used much more loosely to describe a situation of tight credit conditions in general. Of course, prevailing credit conditions are likely to have changed during the course of the crisis, with different situations calling for very different policy responses. Research on this topic is still at an early stage, and both the results and their interpretation very much mixed. This box briefly reviews some recent work on this issue.

• A survey of some 1,200 manufacturing firms in Thailand was undertaken in the last quarter of 1997 and first quarter of 1998, by Dollar and Hallward-Driemeier (1998). Asked to rank the causes of the current output decline (out of four possibilities), the most important factor cited by both exporters and nonexporters was the effect of the exchange rate depreciation on input costs, followed by lack of domestic (or foreign) demand. The high cost of capital was ranked third, and lack of access to credit ranked last.

• Domaç and Ferri (1998) examine the relationship between increases in the spread between bank lending rates and treasury bond rates, and industrial production in Korea. (They also decompose this spread into various interest rates to examine different channels of effects.) In general, they find Granger causality from increases in the spread to subsequent declines in industrial production, and find that a 1 percentage point increase in the overall bank lending spread is associated with a 1.4 percent decline in industrial production (or 1.7 percent in the case of small- and medium-scale enterprises). As such, the paper concludes that wider spreads and higher interest rates could account for a fall in industrial production of as much as 5–10 percent.

While their evidence is suggestive, there are issues in the interpretation of their results. Most important, the estimation period covers the early 1990s through February 1998. Since the variables examined fluctuated relatively little in the sample period until the crisis period—when there was a sharp fall in production and a rise in interest rates—and since no allowance is made for other factors influencing production (such as falling domestic and foreign demand or the effects of exchange rate depreciation—as the Dollar and Hallward-Driemeier evidence suggests), the effect attributed to larger spreads and higher interest rates is necessarily substantial. Moreover, Granger causality says little about economic causality—especially in this context. If output is expected to fall (for whatever reason), the perceived riskiness of lending to the corporate sector would increase, and—assuming even minimal rationality on the part of

capital markets—this should be reflected in an immediate increase in spreads and interest rates: Granger causality here could reflect nothing more than financial variables moving more quickly than the real economy.

• In the debate on whether priority should have been given to stabilizing the exchange rate or lowering interest rates, Claessens, Djankov, and Ferri (1998) assess the impact of the currency and interest rate shocks (between early 1997 and September 1998) on the liquidity of a sample of firms in Indonesia, Korea, Malaysia, the Philippines, and Thailand and on their solvency. They define a firm to be illiquid when earnings (before income tax but after depreciation) fall short of debt service; and insolvent when total liabilities at the new exchange and interest rates exceed end-1996 equity. Given the magnitude of the exchange rate movements, they find that the exchange rate shock alone was sufficient to drive almost two-thirds of Indonesian firms, 20 percent of Korean firms, and 10 percent of Thai firms (in their sample) into insolvency (and 72 percent, 38 percent, and 55 percent, respectively, into illiquidity). The effect of interest rates is rather smaller, with the interest rate shock driving about 2–5 percent of firms in each of the countries into insolvency, and 15 to 25 percent into illiquidity. (The paper also notes, however, that about 35 percent of firms in these countries are solvent but illiquid—suggesting the importance of restoring credit flows rapidly.) The results are analytically interesting, but since the authors do not estimate an explicit trade-off between higher interest rates and a smaller depreciation, the direct operational implications of their findings are, perhaps, somewhat limited.

• Finally, Ghosh and Ghosh (1999) examine whether there was a credit crunch—whereby the (often low or negative) real interest rates may not have cleared the credit market and there was quantity rationing. They apply an explicit disequilibrium framework, and estimate credit supply and credit demand functions. In Indonesia, they find some evidence of a credit crunch in late 1997 as the banking crisis deepened. Thereafter, credit demand also fell sharply so supply was no longer the binding constraint. In Korea and Thailand, they find that, although real credit supply did decrease in late 1997 and early 1998, the fall in real credit demand was sharper, so credit supply was *not* the constraining factor. (These results are thus very much consistent with the findings of Dollar and Hallward-Driemeier (1998) who found, in Thailand, that lack of access to credit was ranked last among factors accounting for the depressed activity.)

There are two important caveats to their results, however. First, rising real interest rates themselves may have contributed to corporate sector distress, quite aside from any credit crunch. Second, the results pertain to the aggregate economy—at a microeconomic level, there may have been (otherwise creditworthy) firms, especially small- and medium-scale enterprises, that were denied credit in an environment of informational asymmetries, and as banks strove to improve loan portfolios and meet capital adequacy standards.

Table 6.2. Required Monetary Contraction to Offset Given Risk Premium Shocks

	Indonesia	Korea	Malaysia	Philippines	Thailand
Parameter estimates					
Interest elasticity	−1.69	−0.40	−2.90	−0.91	−1.91
t-statistic	(−2.65)	(−0.66)	(−2.04)	(−1.78)	(−3.74)
Constant	−2.19	−1.39	−0.97	−1.83	−1.18
t-statistic	(27.90)	(9.86)	(16.29)	(25.48)	(24.69)
Time trend	0.06	0.01	0.04	0.04	0.05
t-statistic	(19.28)	(3.57)	(25.33)	(13.68)	(30.62)
R^2	0.95	0.74	0.96	0.88	0.97
Baseline					
Broad money/GDP, 1996 (in percent)	52.1	45.7	99.4	53.8	81.0
Interest rate, 1996 (in percent a year)	14.0	7.5	7.3	9.7	10.5
Broad money/GDP in 1997 (in percent)	55.6	46.2	103.4	56.3	84.8
Percentage growth, 1997 over 1996	6.5	1.1	4.0	4.5	4.7
Shocks					
Risk premium shock	5.0	5.0	5.0	5.0	5.0
Broad money/GDP in 1997 (in percent)	51.7	45.4	90.6	54.0	78.0
Broad money/GDP 1997/1996 (growth in percent)	−0.9	−0.7	−8.9	0.3	−3.8
Risk premium shock	10.0	10.0	10.0	10.0	10.0
Broad money/GDP in 1997 (in percent)	48.2	44.6	79.8	52.0	71.9
Broad money/GDP 1997/1996 (growth in percent)	−7.6	−2.4	−19.7	−3.5	−11.2

Sources: International Monetary Fund, *International Financial Statistics*; and IMF staff estimates.

parity condition (including a risk premium).[28] The exchange rate is then given by:

$$e(t) = \frac{1}{1+\beta} \sum_{j=0}^{\infty} (\frac{\beta}{1+\beta})^j (m_{t+j} - \alpha y_{t+j} + \beta \pi_{t+j} - v_{t+j}). \quad (1)$$

According to equation (1), the exchange rate depreciates with an increase in the money supply, a slowdown in activity, an increase in the risk premium, or a decrease in the rate of real appreciation.

The initial crisis is perhaps best modeled as an increase in the risk premium, π.[29] There is, of course, no reason to suppose that the increase in

risk premiums was equal across countries. The increase in the risk premium for any individual country reflects investors' perceptions about the design and implementation of the reform programs, the likelihood that other investors will remain in the market, and the prospects of continued servicing of external obligations. Nonetheless, a useful exercise is to consider the required monetary contraction to stabilize the exchange rate for a given shock to the risk premium.

Table 6.2 reports the result of such a simulation. For a given shock to the risk premium (10 percentage points), the table reports the contraction in broad money/GDP required to offset the shock. For instance, given trend increases, the ratio of broad money/GDP would have risen from 0.52 in 1996 to 0.56 in 1997. With a 10 percentage point shock to the risk premium, and given the estimated interest elasticity of money demand of −1.69 (*t*-stat. 2.65**), the ratio of broad money/GDP would need to *decline* to 0.48 (that is, a 7.6 percent decline relative to 1996), if the exchange rate is to be constant. Similar calculations can be done for each of the countries, under an assumed risk premium shock. The required contractions depend primarily on the estimated interest elasticity of money demand, which is negative

---

[28]The standard monetary model is given by

$$m - p = \alpha y - \beta i$$
$$i = i^* + e(t+1) - e(t) + \pi(t)$$
$$p = p^* + e + v,$$

where variables (except i and i^*) are measured in logs, $\pi(t)$ is the risk premium (reflecting both country and currency risk), and v is the real exchange rate. Without loss of generality, i^* and p^* are set equal to 0 in deriving equation (1).

[29]For simplicity, it is assumed that the shock to the risk premium occurs only in the first year. To the extent that the risk premium increase extends over several years, the current (or expected future) monetary contraction must be greater.

Table 6.3. Pass-Through Coefficients and Implied Expected Real Overnight Rates

	Indonesia	Korea	Thailand
Constant	0.00	0.00	0.00
	(2.15)	(2.51)	(3.50)
$\Delta\log(p(-1))$	0.24	0.36	0.07
	(1.80)	(3.25)	(0.71)
$\Delta\log(m(-1))$	0.05	0.05	−0.04
	(1.19)	(1.69)	(−0.82)
$\Delta\log(m(-2))$	0.01	−0.01	−0.02
	(0.36)	(−0.34)	(−0.32)
$\Delta\log(m(-3))$	0.00	0.00	−0.01
	(−0.17)	(−0.04)	(−0.11)
Sum of money coefficients	0.05	0.04	−0.06
$\Delta\log(e(-1))$	0.00	0.03	0.04
	(−0.21)	(1.72)	(0.89)
$\Delta\log(e(-2))$	0.09	0.04	−0.01
	(2.53)	(4.92)	(0.49)
$\Delta\log(e(-3))$	0.01	−0.03	0.03
	(0.19)	(3.85)	(1.46)
Sum of exchange rate coefficients	0.09	0.04	0.05
R^2	0.20	0.42	0.10
	(In percent a year)		
Expected real overnight rates			
1997:Q4	−2.5	6.7	4.2
1998:Q1	5.5	1.1	5.9

Source: IMF staff estimates.

and statistically significant (at least) at the 10 percent level in each of the countries except Korea.

The required contraction in the money/GDP ratio need not, of course, come through a contraction in the nominal money supply. To the extent that there is inflation, part of the contraction will take place through an adjustment of prices.[30] Inasmuch as output is contracting, however, the real monetary contraction would need to be correspondingly *greater*.

Finally, it is worth noting that equation (1) also provides a convenient framework for analyzing the plausibility of a monetary contraction leading to a *depreciation* of the exchange rate. Quite simply, the direct effects of the monetary contraction would need to be outweighed by the indirect effect on money demand through the activity term. Since the income elasticity is typically in the range of 0.5–1.0, this means that a 1 percent monetary contraction would

need to contract output by more than 1 percent, or there would need to be an adverse effect on the risk premium (controlling for any effects on output). Since output elasticities with respect to money are typically well below unity, a monetary contraction would have a perverse effect on the exchange rate only if it resulted in a significant widening of the risk premium.

Expected Real Interest Rates

Real interest rates were measured using an estimate of the contemporaneous rate of inflation. Also of interest is a more forward-looking approach. To estimate expected real interest rates, some means of forecasting price dynamics must be developed; the approach adopted here is perhaps the simplest. For each country, a distributed lag model relating current inflation to lagged inflation, lagged exchange rate changes, and lagged broad money growth is estimated:

$$\Delta\log(p_t^c) = \alpha + \rho\Delta\log(p_{t-1}^c) + \sum_{j=1}^{k}\beta_j\Delta\log(e_{t-j}) + \sum_{j=1}^{k}\gamma_j\,\Delta\log(m_{t-j}). \quad (2)$$

[30]In terms of equation (1), this would be captured by an increase in the real exchange rate, v, which would reflect higher inflation for a given nominal exchange rate.

Table 6.4. Effect on GDP Growth of a Decrease in Money Growth
(In percent a year, at annualized rates)

	Indonesia	Korea	Malaysia	Philippines	Thailand
	Effects of a 10 percentage point decrease in real money growth in year 0 only				
Effect on:					
GDP growth in year 0	−0.3	−2.9	−1.6	−1.0	−0.9
GDP growth in year 1	−1.0	−0.9	−1.7	−0.3	−0.8
GDP growth in year 2	−0.5	0.0	−0.7	−0.1	−0.5
GDP growth in year 3	−0.2	0.0	−0.2	0.0	−0.3
GDP growth in year 4	−0.1	0.0	−0.1	0.0	−0.1
GDP growth in year 5	0.0	0.0	0.0	0.0	−0.1
	Effects of a 10 percentage point decrease in real money growth in quarter 0 only				
Effect on:					
GDP growth in quarter 0	...	−2.6	...	−2.3	...
GDP growth in quarter 1	...	−2.5	...	−0.8	...
GDP growth in quarter 2	...	0.4	...	−0.5	...
GDP growth in quarter 3	...	−2.5	...	−0.1	...
GDP growth in quarter 4	...	−0.2	...	0.0	...
GDP growth in quarter 5	...	0.0	...	0.0	...

Source: IMF staff estimates based on one-year and four-quarter vector autoregressions; estimated over the period 1972–96.

Parameter estimates, using monthly data for the period 1990–97, are reported in the top panel of Table 6.3 (with heteroscedastic-consistent t-statistics reported in parentheses). The autoregressive parameter is generally significant, and exchange rate depreciations feed into higher inflation with a one-to-two month lag. The estimated equations are then used to generate inflation forecasts—and corresponding expected real interest rates, which are reported in the bottom panel of Table 6.3.

Impact of a Monetary Contraction on Real GDP Growth

As discussed earlier, unrestricted vector autoregressions of real GDP growth and real money growth may provide basic insight into the possible effects of monetary tightening. For each of five Asian economies, Table 6.4 reports estimated impulse response functions of real GDP growth to a hypothetical decrease of 10 percentage points in the growth rate of real money (estimated over the period 1972–96). Such a decrease in real money growth is estimated to lower the current rate of GDP growth by about 1 percentage point in Thailand and the Philippines, by 1½ percentage points in Malaysia, and by 3 percentage points in Korea. In Indonesia, the main effect occurs with a one-year lag: growth in the current year falls by only 0.3 percentage point, but in the following year it falls by 1 percentage point. If such estimates are interpreted as causal

elasticities, they can be applied to the observed decelerations of real money balances to yield the estimated growth effects discussed earlier.

Impulse response functions based on quarterly data for Korea and the Philippines give broadly similar results. It is estimated that a 10 percentage point reduction in the growth rate of real money for a single quarter would lower GDP growth in Korea by about 2.5 percentage points (at annualized rates) in the current quarter and the first quarter following the monetary tightening; the estimated effects are somewhat smaller in the Philippines, but cumulatively over the year are of roughly the same magnitude. (Quarterly GDP data are not available for the other countries.)

References

Clasessens, Stijn, Simeon Djankov, and Giovanni Ferri, 1998, "Corporate Distress in East Asia: Assessing the Impact of Interest and Exchange Rate Shocks" (unpublished; Washington: World Bank).

Dollar, David, and Mary Hallward-Driemeier, 1998, "Crisis, Adjustment, and Reform in Thai Industry" (unpublished; Washington: World Bank).

Domaç, Ilker, and Giovanni Ferri, 1998, "The Real Impact of Financial Shocks: Evidence from Korea (unpublished; Washington: World Bank)

Enoch, Charles, and Anne-Marie Gulde, 1997, "Making a Currency Board Operational," IMF Paper on Policy Analysis and Assessment No. 97/10 (Washington: International Monetary Fund).

Furman, Jason, and Joseph Stiglitz, 1998, "Economic Crises: Evidence and Insights from East Asia," paper prepared for the Brookings Panel on Economic Activity (Washington, November).

Ghosh, Atish R., Anne-Marie Gulde, and Holger C. Wolf, 1998, "Currency Boards: The Ultimate Fix?" IMF Working Paper No. 98/8 (Washington: International Monetary Fund).

Ghosh, Swati R., and Atish R. Ghosh, 1999, "East Asia in the Aftermath: Was There a Crunch?" IMF Working Paper No. 99/38 (Washington: International Monetary Fund).

Goldfajn, Ilan, and Taimur Baig, 1998, "Monetary Policy in the Aftermath of Currency Crises: The Case of Asia," IMF Working Paper No. 98/170 (Washington: International Monetary Fund).

Goldfajn, Ilan, and Poonam Gupta, 1998, "Does Tight Monetary Policy Stabilize the Exchange Rate?" (unpublished; Washington: International Monetary Fund).

Kraay, Aardt, 1998, "Do High Interest Rates Defend Currencies During Speculative Attacks?" (unpublished; Washington: World Bank).

Lebergott, Stanley, 1984, *The Americans: An Economic Record* (New York: W.W. Norton).

Molho, Lazaros, 1994, "Fiscal Adjustment in an Oil-Exporting Country: The Case of Indonesia," IMF Paper on Policy Analysis and Assessment No. 94/21 (Washington: International Monetary Fund).

Santiprabhob, Veerathai, 1997, "Bank Soundness and Currency Board Arrangements: Issues and Experience," IMF Paper on Policy Analysis and Assessment No. 97/11 (Washington: International Monetary Fund).

VII Fiscal Policy

Timothy Lane and Tsidi Tsikata

The role envisaged for fiscal policy in the Asian crisis countries has shifted with the changing assessment of the economic situation. The initial programs in all three countries included some measure of fiscal adjustment to counter an initial deterioration of fiscal positions, with a view to contributing to current account adjustment and thus avoiding an excessive squeeze on the private sector, as well as building room for noninflationary financing of carrying costs of financial sector restructuring. To the extent that fiscal adjustment made credible steps toward these objectives, it was expected to contribute to restoring confidence. This fiscal adjustment was intended to be comparatively mild in Indonesia and Korea, whereas it was stronger in Thailand where the initial current account deficit was significantly larger, as was the previous deterioration of the fiscal position. These fiscal programs were, of course, formulated in a context where the slowdown in economic growth was—as it turned out, mistakenly—expected to be relatively modest (see Section IV above).[1]

Beginning in early 1998, as the severity of the economic downturn became apparent, and while external current accounts shifted into large surpluses owing to declining domestic demand and large currency depreciations, fiscal deficits were programmed to expand considerably in all three countries. Fiscal policy became increasingly oriented toward supporting economic activity as the programs evolved. In the initial programs and early reviews, fiscal policies had sought to limit the deterioration of the fiscal position associated with the automatic stabilizers and the effects of exchange rate depreciations. Beginning early in 1998, they shifted to accommodating part of the effect of economic conditions on fiscal balances, and, subsequently to augmenting these effects through expansionary measures. It has proved difficult, however, for the authorities—especially in Indonesia and Korea—to move quickly to make full use of the scope for expansionary fiscal action allowed under the program ceilings.

This section reviews the fiscal policy content of the programs, first discussing the rationale for fiscal adjustment in the initial programs, next describing what was done in the programs, and finally assessing the appropriateness of the fiscal stance, both in the initial programs and in the wake of the successive revisions prompted by changing economic circumstances.

Initial Rationale for Fiscal Adjustment

Fiscal deficits were not viewed as a major concern in these countries for much of the period leading up to the crisis. Indeed (as discussed in Section II above), the crises were mainly "made in the private sector," reflecting financial sector vulnerabilities rather than the more conventional situation of monetization of fiscal deficits. Conventionally measured central government balances in all three countries were in surplus or at most slightly in deficit throughout the 1990s up until 1996 (see Figure 2.5 above). The strong fiscal positions reflected, in part, fiscal consolidation efforts in the late 1980s (Indonesia and Thailand) or earlier (Korea).[2] As fiscal positions improved and growth continued to be strong, the ratio of public debt to GDP had been falling in all three countries.

However, even if fiscal imbalances were not a major part of the problem, that did not necessarily mean that fiscal adjustment could not be part of an appropriate solution. Public savings could contribute to the overall current account adjustment dictated by the reversal of capital flows and, by boosting confidence, could influence the total amount of external adjustment required. A wider fiscal deficit, if financed domestically, could crowd out financing to the private sector. In addition, the costs of financial sector restructuring needed to be met.

---

[1]The coverage of the fiscal accounts used for the programs differs across the three countries as described in Appendix 7.1.

[2]For discussions of fiscal sustainability and fiscal adjustment, see Bascand and Razin (1997) and Molho (1994) on Indonesia and Kochhar and others (1996) on Thailand.

External Adjustment

The programs were formulated against the background of the sharp reversal of international capital inflows associated with the crisis. The programs sought to reduce the need for current account adjustment associated with these capital outflows by providing official financing and restoring confidence to encourage a recovery of private sector flows. In this setting, fiscal adjustment, particularly in Thailand, was intended to play two roles: minimizing the need for external adjustment by helping restore confidence quickly; and balancing the composition of the unavoidable current account adjustment between public and private sectors.[3]

Fiscal adjustment can have positive effects on confidence mainly to the extent that it is expected to have effects on investors' prospects of repayment. To the extent that fiscal adjustment has positive effects on the external current account and thus reduces the need for currency depreciation, it would tend to reduce both the expectation of currency depreciation and country risk premiums. Moreover, as reducing fiscal deficits also reduces the likelihood of their monetization, this would tend to lower expectations of inflation and currency depreciation. Excessively harsh fiscal adjustment could, in principle, have the opposite effect, to the extent that market participants expected it to result in a contraction of economic activity that would worsen their prospects of repayment.

The initial programs envisaged a relatively minor current account adjustment, and a correspondingly small contribution of public saving to this adjustment (Figure 7.1) in the context of a modest and short-lived slowdown in economic growth. In Indonesia, the current account was expected to adjust by only about ¾ of 1 percentage point of GDP from 1996/97 through the end of the program, of which about ¼ of 1 percentage point was to reflect an improved government balance. Korea's current account adjustment from 1997 through the end of the program was projected at 2¾ percentage points of GDP, of which public saving was to account for about ¼ of 1 percentage point. In Thailand, where the initial current account imbalances were largest, the current account balance was to adjust by only 1½ percentage points from 1996/97 through the end of the program, while the programmed improvement in the public sector balance was about 1¼ percentage points of GDP.

There is a stark contrast between the adjustment originally envisaged and the way the programs actually unfolded. In contrast to the original picture of fiscal policy helping along a modest current account adjustment, the latest reviews show a large ex post fiscal easing set against massive current account adjustments imposed by market forces. Underlying this latter set of projections, of course, is the sharp drop in output and demand and greater-than-expected currency depreciations, which strengthened the current account and weakened the fiscal position in all three countries.

Financing

Corresponding to the adjustments in sectoral savings-investment balances just discussed is the distribution of financing that is the focus of the IMF's standard financial programming framework. The fiscal position determines credit to government when other sources of funding are given. This in turn—when set against paths for money and domestic credit that are estimated to be consistent with given assumptions about growth and inflation and targets for international reserves—determines the room available for credit to nongovernment.[4] For this reason, fiscal adjustment is typically needed to permit the other objectives of the program to be achieved without unduly compressing credit to nongovernment. By the same token, any slippage in achieving the fiscal targets tends to require either a reduction of credit to the private sector, an unprogrammed increase in money creation, or both. This analysis of financing flows is the counterpart of the current account adjustment just discussed.

In the Asian programs under review, the composition of financing of government deficits has been changing as the programs have evolved: domestic financing of fiscal deficits has ballooned while resource transfers from abroad have dropped. The composition of financing as of the most recent review,[5] presented in Table 7.1, suggests that in Korea and Thailand, the deficit is now largely domestically financed, so the fiscal deficit has a direct negative effect on the credit available to the private sector. In Indonesia, in contrast, the balanced budget law dictates that deficits should be entirely externally financed, and changes to fiscal policy have been configured with that constraint in mind.[6]

---

[3]Appendix 7.2 illustrates this point in the context of a variant of the Mundell-Fleming model.

[4]Of course, in a broader context, fiscal policy would itself affect growth and inflation, partially offsetting the effects discussed in this section.

[5]For Indonesia, the second review; for Korea, the third quarterly review; and for Thailand, the fourth review.

[6]This does not, of course, rule out the possibility that financing of the public sectors would partly crowd out financing to the private sector.

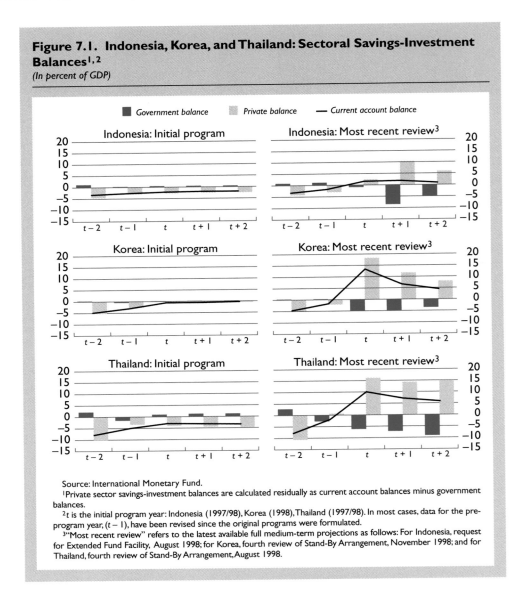

Figure 7.1. Indonesia, Korea, and Thailand: Sectoral Savings-Investment Balances[1,2]

(In percent of GDP)

Source: International Monetary Fund.

[1]Private sector savings-investment balances are calculated residually as current account balances minus government balances.

[2]t is the initial program year: Indonesia (1997/98), Korea (1998), Thailand (1997/98). In most cases, data for the pre-program year, $(t-1)$, have been revised since the original programs were formulated.

[3]"Most recent review" refers to the latest available full medium-term projections as follows: For Indonesia, request for Extended Fund Facility, August 1998; for Korea, fourth review of Stand-By Arrangement, November 1998; and for Thailand, fourth review of Stand-By Arrangement, August 1998.

Bank Restructuring

Another reason for fiscal adjustment in the initial programs was to make room for costs of bank restructuring, which was to include closing nonviable banks and injecting public funds to recapitalize some viable ones.[7] The budgetary impact of banking sector restructuring is conventionally represented by its carrying costs, recently estimated at 3 percent of GDP for Thailand, 1½ percent for Indonesia, and ¾ of 1 percent for Korea in the current fiscal year; these costs are expected to rise to about 2 percentage points of GDP in Indonesia and over 2 percentage points of GDP in Korea in the medium term (see Appendix 7.3).

The budgetary treatment of bank restructuring differed across the three countries. In Indonesia and Korea, it was intended to be supported by the government directly,[8] while in Thailand such support was initially provided indirectly by the central bank, with only a small proportion of estimated fiscal costs having been brought explicitly into the budget. The

---

[7]The financial sector restructuring is discussed in greater detail in Section VIII below.

[8]In practice, as discussed elsewhere (Sections VI and VIII) the banks in Indonesia were also provided with large amounts of central bank liquidity support. This is not included in the bank restructuring costs reported here.

Table 7.1. Financing of Fiscal Deficits¹
(Percent of total financing)

	Indonesia	Korea	Thailand
Domestic	0.0	69.0	88.7
Privatization	15.8	—	—
Foreign	84.2	31.0	11.3

¹First full program year (Indonesia, 1998/99; Korea, 1998; and Thailand, 1997/98).

modes of financing bank restructuring programs have included government-guaranteed bonds (Indonesia and Korea) and short-term borrowing from the money market and the central bank (Thailand).

The economic impact of bank recapitalization depends on several factors. If the losses incurred by the banks had been completely unexpected and had occurred in the current fiscal year, or if a government bailout had not previously been expected, the operation would entail a one-time capital outlay and a perpetual stream of carrying costs on such bonds. Alternatively, if all the banks' losses had been preexisting and if it had been common knowledge that they would be covered by a government guarantee, these capital and carrying costs should have entered into an assessment of the fiscal position in economic terms as soon as the loan losses were incurred (that is, before as well as after the operation), not when the operation was carried out. In this case, since carrying out the operation itself only converts an implicit claim on the government into an explicit one, its immediate monetary and fiscal impact would, as a first approximation, be zero.[9]

In the Asian crisis countries, the situation was obviously somewhere between these two extremes: implicit government guarantees were pervasive but their precise coverage was uncertain; and, while it was common knowledge that financial institutions had some poor quality loans, the crisis both revealed the magnitude of these loans and led many

more loans to turn nonperforming. The assessment of the overall impact of fiscal policy below will follow common practice in using, as the central case, the assumption that the fiscal impact of restructuring is approximated by its carrying costs—while noting the possibility that carrying out restructuring could have either a smaller or a larger expansionary effect.

What Was Done?

Original Programs

Based on the considerations discussed, the original IMF-supported programs in the Asian crisis countries incorporated some element of fiscal adjustment. The most meaningful way of characterizing the adjustment in economic terms is with regard to the change in the fiscal balance compared with the previous year. This year-on-year change can be broken down into a part attributable to discretionary fiscal policy and another part that is a passive response to changing economic conditions—economic activity, the exchange rate, and other factors (including oil prices, in the case of Indonesia). In contrast the "headline" amounts of fiscal adjustment, reported when the programs were announced, are defined in relation to a baseline implied by the authorities' unchanged plans. The decomposition based on the actual change in the fiscal balance from one year to the next gives a clearer picture of the economic impact of fiscal policies than the headline numbers, which focus on revisions to plans that, in the end, were never implemented.

The magnitude of fiscal adjustment based on the "headline" measure is shown on line 2 in Table 7.2. The intended fiscal adjustment was largest for Thailand—2.1 percent of GDP in the first full fiscal year of the program, including carrying costs of bank restructuring, or 3.2 percentage points excluding those carrying costs. The reason for larger fiscal adjustment in Thailand was that initial fiscal and external imbalances were larger there than in the other two countries. The programmed adjustment was smaller in Indonesia (1.1 percentage points of GDP including, or 1.6 percentage points excluding, bank restructuring) and Korea (0.8 percentage points including, or 1.6 percentage points excluding, bank restructuring). In light of the assumption of a relatively moderate slowdown of economic growth, these planned adjustments were modest.

A decomposition of the year-on-year change in the fiscal balance—the more economically meaningful measure—gives a somewhat different picture, as

---

[9]Bank restructuring can also have an economic impact through several other channels: it may eliminate moral hazard problems associated with allowing insolvent institutions to continue in business; it may transfer wealth to banks' depositors, other creditors, and/or owners; depending on how it is financed, it may affect the money supply; and, under some circumstances, it may lead to a narrowing of bank interest rate spreads. See Daniel and Saal (1997) and Lane (1996). In principle, it would be preferable to record the capital costs of the restructuring using an augmented balance approach; see Daniel, Davis, and Wolfe (1997).

Table 7.2. Fiscal Policy in Original Programs
(In percent of GDP)

| | Indonesia[1] | | Korea[2] | Thailand[3] |
	1997/98	1998/99	1998	1997/98
1. Overall balance (level)	0.3	0.5	0.2	−0.1
2. Change compared with				
no-measures baseline[4]	0.6	1.1	0.8	2.1
Revenue[5]	0.1	0.0	0.8	1.2
Expenditure[5]	−1.0	−1.6	−0.8	−1.6
Financial restructuring	0.5	0.5	0.8	1.1
Other[6]	—	—	—	0.4
3. Change compared with previous year	−0.9	0.2	0.2	1.0
Due to economic environment	−1.3	0.3	−0.4	−0.9
Due to policy changes	0.3	0.2	−0.1	1.9
Of which:				
Financial restructuring	−0.5	0.0	−0.8	−1.1
Residual	0.2	−0.2	0.7	0.0
4. *Memorandum item:*				
GDP growth (percent a year)[7]	5.0	3.0	2.5	3.5

[1]Central government. Fiscal year: April 1–March 31.
[2]Consolidated central government. Fiscal year: January 1–December 31.
[3]Public sector. Fiscal year: October 1–September 30.
[4]No measures baseline and program targets are based on the macroeconomic projections made at the time of the original programs.
[5]For Thailand, refers to the central government.
[6]For Thailand, adjustment implicit in the accounts of the non-central-government public sector.
[7]Original program projections; nearest calendar year.

shown in Table 7.3.[10] The original programs envisaged some year-to-year improvement in the fiscal balance in Korea and Thailand, while in Indonesia, policies aimed from the outset at containing an expected deterioration. In Indonesia, the fiscal position was projected to deteriorate by 0.9 percentage point of GDP in 1997/98 and improve by 0.2 percentage point in 1998/99. In Korea, the programmed improvement in the fiscal balance was small (0.2 percent of GDP in fiscal 1998). In Thailand, the fiscal balance was projected to improve by 1 percentage point of GDP during fiscal 1997/98, thus recovering about one-third of the sharp deterioration then expected for fiscal 1996/97. Even in Thailand, the programmed tightening was not particularly large in relation to other IMF-supported programs,[11] and of a

similar order of magnitude to adjustments of some major industrial countries at various times in the 1990s. In Indonesia and Korea, the overall planned adjustment was even smaller.

The envisaged and actual changes in fiscal positions reflect a combination of economic environment and policy changes. Economic conditions—the projected slowdown of growth and exchange rate depreciation—were expected to weaken fiscal positions in all three countries. Policy changes in Indonesia's initial program were intended to improve the 1997/98 fiscal position by 0.3 percentage point of GDP—and a further 0.2 percentage point in 1998/99—with about two-thirds of the impact on the spending side. (Part of the projected improvement in revenue was associated with unspecified revenue measures that, in the event, were never implemented.)[12] In Korea, the net effect of policy changes in 1998 was expected to be slightly expansionary, weakening the fiscal position

[10]The underlying analysis of fiscal positions, undertaken by the staff of the IMF's Fiscal Affairs Department, is also summarized in International Monetary Fund (1998), Box 6.2.

[11]By way of comparison, in the IMF's Stand-By and Extended Arrangements during 1988–92 the average change in the actual fiscal balance over the life of the program was estimated at about 3 percentage points of GDP. See Bennett and others (1995).

[12]The methodology used defines a neutral fiscal position in terms of an unchanged tax structure and an unchanged ratio of expenditures to GDP (for a given exchange rate).

Table 7.3. Sources of Changes in the Fiscal Balance
(In percent of GDP; a negative number indicates a fiscal deterioration)

	Indonesia[1]				Korea[2]				Thailand[3]			
	Original		Recent[4]		Original		Recent[4]		Original		Recent[4]	
	1997/98	1998/99	1997/98	1998/99	1997	1998	1997	1998	1996/97	1997/98	1996/97	1997/98
Fiscal balance (level)[5]	0.3	0.5	-0.9	-10.1	0.0	0.2	0.0	-5.0	-1.1	-0.1	-1.6	-5.1
Change in fiscal balance												
Change due to economic environment	-0.9	0.2	-2.2	-9.2	...	-0.8	...	-5.0	-3.3	1.0	-4.0	-3.5
Exchange rate[6]	-1.3	0.3	-4.2	-11.1	...	-0.4	...	-1.9	-1.1	-0.9	-0.3	-3.1
GDP growth	-1.4	0.2	-3.5	-6.4	...	-0.3	...	-0.9	-0.2	-0.9	-0.2	-2.0
Oil price	-0.2	0.1	-0.5	-0.7	...	-0.1	...	-1.0	-1.0	0.0	-0.1	-0.9
Policy changes												
Outlays	0.3	0.2	2.7	1.7	...	0.0	...	-2.8	-1.2	1.9	-2.6	-0.6
Social safety net[7]	0.2	0.4	2.7	3.8	...	-0.1	...	-1.1	-0.6	1.8	-1.9	2.6
Bank restructuring	0.0	0.0	0.0	-1.0	...	0.1	...	-2.1	-0.6	0.0	0.0	-0.6
Statutory revenue change	0.6	-0.2	0.0	-1.6	...	0.8	...	1.8	0.0	-1.1	-0.7	-2.0
Residual (unexplained)	0.2	-0.2	0.7	0.5	...	0.7	...	-0.4	-1.0	0.0	-1.1	0.1
Memorandum items:												
Nominal GDP growth rate	13.2	13.1	19.8	43.4	7.9	6.6	7.9	0.1	10.1	11.3	6.1	5.3
Real GDP growth rate	5.0	3.0	4.6	-12.1	5.5	2.5	5.5	-7.0	2.5	3.5	-0.4	-5.0

[1] For Indonesia, the first fiscal year considered as "program year" is 1997/98 (April 1997–March 1998).
[2] For Korea, the first fiscal year considered as "program year" is 1998 (January 1998–December 1998).
[3] For Thailand, the first fiscal year considered as "program year" is 1997/98 (October 1997–September 1998).
[4] Calculations as of July 1998.
[5] This measure of the balance excludes privatization proceeds, but includes bank restructuring costs.
[6] For Indonesia, the exchange rate effects are in real rather than nominal terms.
[7] This excludes the effect of exchange rate changes on subsidies arising from the failure to fully adjust commodity prices. These effects are included above as effects from "economic conditions."

by 0.1 percent of GDP. Spending cuts and revenue increases were expected to less than offset the carrying costs of bank restructuring. The projected overall improvement in the fiscal position in Korea is due to the large positive "residual" (0.7 percentage point of GDP), which in this case appears mainly to reflect optimistic revenue projections (overly optimistic, as it now appears) for given macroeconomic assumptions and tax structure. In Thailand, it was recognized that policies had likely added to the fiscal weakening in 1996/97. For 1997/98 (the first full program year) policy measures were intended to improve the fiscal balance by 1.9 percent of GDP, with spending reductions and revenue increases partly offset by the costs of bank restructuring.

Thus, the policy measures included in the original programs, had they been implemented in the macroeconomic environment expected at the time, would have implied a deterioration in the fiscal balance in Indonesia, a very small improvement in Korea, and a more significant, yet far from drastic, improvement in Thailand relative to the expected outcome for the previous fiscal year. These figures suggest that the "headline" figures presented earlier (as well as in staff assessments and public announcements) gave an exaggerated picture of the fiscal adjustment effort. The key difference is that the headline figures record intended changes *from the authorities' previous plans*, while the figures in Table 7.3 record intended changes in policy *from year to year*.

Revisions and Current Prospects

The thrust of fiscal policy in the Asian crisis countries turned out to be substantially different from that originally expected. This was chiefly because of radical revisions to the original assumptions for economic growth, capital flows, and exchange rates.[13] Both economic activity and exchange rates had major direct effects on fiscal balances, to which policies had to respond when the programs were reviewed.

Fiscal targets in IMF-supported programs (which may or may not be embodied in formal performance criteria) are typically projections based on current policies and assumptions together with measures adopted under the programs; in the Asian crisis countries, these assumptions were proved drastically wrong. The overall result depends on the extent to which either targets were allowed to give way to altered circumstances or policies were strengthened to maintain the targets in the face of more difficult economic conditions. In the Asian crisis countries, program revisions accommodated a substantial part of the expansionary effect of changing economic condi-

tions on the fiscal position from the start of 1998. Later in the programs, revisions went beyond accommodation to incorporate some additional stimulus.

The recession had a substantial effect on fiscal balances, primarily through its negative effect on revenues. Initially, in the absence of formal arrangements for the government to pay unemployment or similar benefits,[14] there was relatively little effect on nominal expenditure levels. Based on program projections at the end of October 1998, the impact of the slowdown in economic activity is expected to be largest in Indonesia, amounting to a cumulative increase in the fiscal deficit of 4½ percentage points of GDP (in 1997/98 and 1998/99). In Korea (1998) and Thailand (1997/98), this contribution to the deficit is expected to amount to 1 percentage point of GDP.

Exchange rate changes also had an important impact on the fiscal balance in these economies. In all three countries, exchange rate depreciation had a substantial negative impact on corporate income tax receipts, as the domestic currency cost of servicing foreign-currency-denominated debt was revalued, lowering corporate taxable income. Foreign exchange gain and loss provisions allowed firms to treat both the interest payments and the increase in domestic currency value of principal repayments on foreign currency debt as an expense. Of lesser importance is the effect on the expenditure side of the increased cost of servicing foreign-currency-denominated public debt.

Another important effect of exchange rate depreciation was that it led to rising outlays on price subsidies on imported goods and increases in the domestic currency cost of government imports. This effect was particularly important in Indonesia, where subsidies on basic food items (notably rice) were increased to keep the rupiah depreciation from resulting in widespread starvation. On the other hand, depreciation boosted domestic currency revenues from taxes imposed on international trade[15]—offset by any contraction in import volumes that occurred.

Taking all these effects together, the depreciations weakened all three countries' fiscal positions substantially. In Korea and Thailand, both revenues and expenditures were adversely affected; whereas in Indonesia, about half of the increase in expenditures as-

---

[13]See Sections IV and V above.

[14]Under the programs, social safety nets were expanded, heightening the sensitivity of government spending to the cycle.

[15]Between 1991 and 1996, the share of international trade taxes in total tax revenues fell from 45 percent to 30 percent in Indonesia (oil and gas revenues dominate these ratios), from 21 percent to 14 percent in Thailand, and from 10 percent to 7 percent in Korea. However, consumption taxes (e.g., excises and VAT), which make up a substantial share of total revenues—30 percent, 38 percent, and 43 percent in Indonesia, Korea, and Thailand, respectively—are quite sensitive to import levels, and so are affected indirectly by exchange rate changes.

sociated with depreciation (mainly on subsidies) was offset by the increase in tax revenues (mainly associated with taxes on oil and gas and on consumption).

As the countries' fiscal positions were weakened substantially by the exchange rate and output movements associated with the crisis, the appropriate response depended on an assessment of the initial situation and the nature of the shocks to economic activity and the exchange rate. To the extent that these shocks were transitory, there would be a case for accommodating them, accepting temporary fiscal imbalances that would be unwound over the medium term. To the extent that they were permanent, some adjustment toward an appropriate medium-term position would be desirable. Although, of course, not all of this adjustment would need to be undertaken in the year the shocks occurred—particularly if this was already a time of grave economic weakness—a credible start with such adjustment would be needed to convince markets and the public that a sound fiscal position would indeed be achieved in the medium term.

The programs assumed that a significant portion of the shocks to real activity were transitory, with a return to growth projected over the medium term.[16] Under these conditions, the appropriate response— both on grounds of stabilizing output fluctuations and of optimal tax smoothing—would be to permit some temporary fiscal easing provided that this easing could be financed.[17] The appropriate *degree* of easing depends on various conditions. In particular, there is nothing necessarily optimal about "letting automatic stabilizers work"—since the sensitivity of the revenues and expenditures to the cycle depends on various features of the tax and expenditure system—for example, the rates and progressivity of personal income tax and the responsiveness of social spending to income (features that vary considerably across countries, and may or may not be set appropriately in a particular case). Thus, policy measures may be needed to augment or partially offset the impact of the cycle on the fiscal position. In particular, in these countries the low sensitivities of expenditures to the cycle and delays in tax collection limit the effectiveness of the automatic stabilizers, suggesting a need for countercyclical policy measures.

The exchange rate depreciations may be assumed to have both a permanent and a transitory component, owing to the assumed need for some real exchange rate adjustment along with a substantial degree of overshooting. It would thus be consistent to assume that some but not all of the changes in revenues and expenditures associated with the depreciations were permanent. The fact that some of the increase in the fiscal deficit resulting from the depreciation was reflected not in increased disposable incomes for domestic residents but in increased debt-service payments abroad, and thus did not contribute to domestic demand, would argue, other things being equal, for a greater degree of accommodation.

Policy changes in successive program revisions in all three countries accommodated a large portion of the automatic easing associated with changing economic conditions. In general, the early reviews entailed partial accommodation, with the exception of the first (November 1997) review of Thailand's program, which (it is now realized, mistakenly) tried to maintain the existing fiscal target by offsetting the full impact of the deteriorating economic situation.[18] In later reviews during the course of 1998, as the severity of the downturn became increasingly evident, fiscal targets in all three countries were revised beyond the automatic effects of economic conditions, to provide a greater stimulus. In some cases, by mid-1998 IMF staff missions also found themselves pressing the authorities to use the room available under existing fiscal targets.[19]

This change in course leads up to the situation in recent months. According to projections based on policies in place at the end of October 1998, fiscal policy measures are projected to have had a net expansionary effect in both Korea (2¾ percentage points of GDP in 1998) and Thailand (0.6 percentage point in 1997/98), over and above the substantial automatic easing resulting from changing economic conditions. In Indonesia, in contrast, where the fiscal balance is programmed to deteriorate much more than in the other countries as a result of the economic situation—notably as a result of increasing fuel and food subsidies in response to exchange rate depreciation—other fiscal policy measures are expected to offset about one-third of this automatic easing.[20]

---

[16]It is also possible that the crisis heralded balance sheet adjustments and major structural changes in these economies that would require several years of low or negative growth to work their way through. Such an assessment, if correct, would call for greater fiscal adjustment.

[17]Tax smoothing, of course, assumes that the government can borrow and lend freely, whereas these economies were constrained in their borrowing during the crisis.

[18]The rationale for this decision at the time was that the new government needed to establish its credibility by standing behind the targets that had previously been agreed with the IMF.

[19]It may therefore turn out that actual fiscal policies have been more contractionary than targeted under the programs. In that case, the economic impact of fiscal policy would need to be reassessed in light of the actual outturns.

[20]These calculations are obviously very sensitive to where one draws the line between economic conditions and policy measures. In particular, if increasing subsidies in response to exchange rate depreciations were defined as measures rather than as a neutral policy of accommodating the efforts of changing economic conditions, Indonesia's fiscal policy would appear 5–6 percentage points of GDP more expansionary than on the basis of the figures presented here.

Assessment

This section has examined how and why the fiscal position changed, both in the initial programs and in the light of subsequent reviews. The original programs contained fiscal measures intended to prevent the fiscal deficit from widening excessively, but were based on the assumption of a relatively moderate economic slowdown and modest currency depreciation. The policy measures in these initial programs would have been far from sufficient to prevent a substantial expansion of fiscal deficits in light of the macroeconomic conditions that actually emerged. In the wake of the program reviews, policy was eased further. As a result, the net effect of policy measures was expansionary in Korea and Thailand. In Indonesia, where the automatic deterioration in the fiscal position was particularly large, policy measures went in the opposite direction, partly offsetting the massive increase in the deficit resulting from the changing economic situation.

These facts contrast sharply with the widespread perception that the IMF applied a standard prescription—harsh fiscal austerity—to a nonstandard situation in all these countries. In part, this is the difference between an analysis based on revisions to fiscal *plans* and one based on changes in fiscal *actions:* in assessing the economic impact, it is obviously more relevant to examine what is actually being done than to examine revisions to plans that were never realized. The impression that the programs kept a tight rein on government budgets also partly reflects the unrealistically optimistic macroeconomic assumptions underlying the initial programs. Such perceptions may also reflect a lack of public understanding of the nature of targets in IMF programs: such targets are not set in stone, but in practice are frequently revised in light of changing economic conditions, in the context of program reviews—and it is the stance taken toward such revisions, as much as the initial program itself, that determines the overall result. It should also be acknowledged that, in the Asian crisis countries, the IMF may be partly responsible for overselling the fiscal adjustment measures in the initial programs with a view to bolstering market confidence.

This leaves the question of whether fiscal policies should have been more supportive of economic activity right from the start. At one level, the answer is clearly "yes": as the severity of the downturn was not adequately taken into account in formulating the initial programs, these programs erred in underestimating the need for fiscal policy to support activity.

However, there are limits to the ability of fiscal policy to support activity in the midst of a currency and banking crisis, associated with a sharp withdrawal of external financing. The crisis implied a tightened external financing constraint that forced massive current account adjustments. These adjustments had to be brought about through some combination of adjustment of the interest rate and exchange rate, and fiscal adjustment. The limited effectiveness of currency depreciation as an expenditure switching policy (given concurrent depreciations in several countries), together with the adverse balance-sheet effects of the exchange rate depreciations themselves, implied that most of the current account adjustment came from a reduction in domestic absorption. In this setting, and given that the effects of an easier fiscal policy on the financing constraint were at best ambiguous, an expansionary fiscal policy at that stage could easily have placed an even larger adjustment burden on the private sector.

From this perspective, fiscal policy begins to have a significant stimulative effect only as external financing constraints are relaxed or as additional external financing becomes available to finance wider fiscal deficits. It was thus appropriate that fiscal policies were eased significantly in early 1998, as market pressures on Korea and Thailand began to ease, while Indonesia obtained foreign official financing for larger deficits. By the same token, if more external financing had been available at the outset, there would have been less need for current account adjustment and more room for fiscal easing to support economic activity.

Appendix 7.1. Coverage of Reported Fiscal Accounts

The coverage of the reported fiscal accounts in *Indonesia* is the narrowest of the three countries; it relates mainly to the operations of the central government. The accounts reflect transfers to lower levels of government and the balances of the two largest extrabudgetary funds. Although local governments are excluded, their deficits beyond those financed by transfers from the central government are estimated to be small. Also excluded are any deficits of the approximately 170 public enterprises.

Two main fiscal balances are reported for *Korea*—the central government balance, and the "consolidated central government" balance. The latter, on which the formal quantitative fiscal targets of the IMF-supported program have been established, consists of the central government and four public enterprises' special accounts. The central government finances are operated through a general account, 18 special accounts (including some for transfers to local governments), and 34 budgetary funds (including the National Pension Fund). The consolidated central government provides only a partial picture of the operations of the public sector, since it only covers a small portion of the operations of local governments and public enterprises (with combined size estimated to be nearly equal to the size of the central government).

Thailand has the broadest coverage of fiscal accounts of the three countries. The reported "consolidated public sector balance" takes account of the operations of the central government, local governments, and nonfinancial public enterprises. However, because of long reporting lags for local government and public enterprise accounts, the formal quantitative fiscal targets in the IMF-supported program relate to the central government balance.

Appendix 7.2. Fiscal Adjustment and Current Account Adjustment

This appendix briefly reviews the simple analytics of fiscal and current account adjustment in a Keynesian fixed-price framework. This simplified framework differs from the standard case of the Mundell-Fleming model in that capital inflows are assumed to be limited, and exchange rate movements are assumed to affect private consumption via wealth effects.

The available policy instruments are assumed to be government spending and the domestic interest rate (for algebraic simplicity, the money market is not modeled explicitly). Output is demand determined, with aggregate demand given by:

$$Y = C(y, e) + I(r)G + CA(y, e),$$

where $0 < C_y < 1$ (marginal propensity to consume is less than unity); $C_e < 0$ (an exchange rate depreciation raises the consumer price index via the price of imported goods and lowers real wealth); $I_r < 0$ (investment is decreasing in the interest rate); $CA_y < 0$ (higher income results in higher imports and a deterioration of the current account); and $CA_e > 0$ (the Marshall-Lerner condition is satisfied).

The country faces capital outflows, which must be financed by a current account surplus:

$$CA(y, e) = F.$$

Totally differentiating, and substituting yields an expression for output, as a function of changes in monetary (r) or fiscal (G) policy, as well as the exogenous outflow (F):

$$dy = \frac{\left[1 + \dfrac{C_e}{CA_e}\right] dF + I_r dr + dG}{\left[1 - C_y + \dfrac{C_e CA_y}{CA_e}\right]}.$$

Correspondingly, the exchange rate is given by

$$de = \frac{1}{(1-C_y) + \dfrac{C_e CA_y}{CA_e}} \left[\frac{dF}{CA_e}(1-C_y-CA_y) - CA_y(I_r dr + dG)\right].$$

From the model, several results drop out:

1. There is a trade-off between interest rates and exchange rates consistent with a given financing constraint:

$$\frac{de}{dr}\Big|_{dF=dG=0} = \frac{-CA_y I_r}{1 - C_y + \dfrac{C_e CA_y}{CA_e}} < 0. \tag{1}$$

A larger volume of capital outflows ($dF > 0$) must be met with a higher interest rate, a more depreciated exchange rate, or both:

$$\frac{de}{dF}\Big|_{dr=dG=0} = \frac{(1 - C_y - CA_y)/CA_e}{1 - C_y + \dfrac{C_e CA_y}{CA_e}} > 0. \tag{2}$$

$$\frac{dr}{dF}\Big|_{de=dG=0} = \frac{(1 - C_y - CA_y)/CA_e}{Ca_y I_r} > 0. \tag{3}$$

Fiscal consolidation ($dG < 0$) permits a lower interest rate and/or a less depreciated exchange rate, consistent with a given volume of capital outflows:

$$\frac{de}{dG}\Big|_{dr=dF=0} = \frac{-CA_y}{1 - C_y + \dfrac{C_e CA_y}{CA_e}} > 0 \tag{4}$$

$$\frac{dr}{dG}\Big|_{de=dF=0} = \frac{-1}{I_r} > 0. \tag{5}$$

As in any Keynesian model, fiscal consolidation lowers aggregate demand and private consumption. With the financing constraint, however, part of the impact of fiscal consolidation is mitigated by the smaller exchange rate depreciation (for given capital outflow):

$$\frac{dC}{dG}\Big|_{dr=dF=0} = \frac{(C_y - C_e CA_y)}{1 - C_y + \dfrac{C_e CA_y}{CA_e}} > 0, \tag{6}$$

where $C_y > 0$, but $-C_e CA_y < 0$.

This result will tend to hold a fortiori if fiscal consolidation ($dG < 0$) results in a smaller capital outflow because of confidence effects ($dF/dG > 0$):

$$\frac{dC}{dG}\Big|_{dr=0} = [(C_y(1 + (1 + C_e/CA_e)dF/dG) \quad (7)$$
$$- C_e CA_y + C_e(1 - C_y - CA_y)$$
$$dF/dG)] / [1 - C_y + (C_e CA_y/CA_e)].$$

Appendix 7.3. Financial Sector Restructuring Costs in the Fiscal Accounts

Indonesia. The costs to the government of restructuring the financial system include compensation to the central bank for past support of failed banks, recapitalization of banks, payments to small depositors, and the operational costs of the bank restructuring agency (IBRA). Direct budgetary transfers and government-guaranteed bonds are the main instruments for delivering government support.

The total stock of bonds to be issued in 1998/99 is estimated at Rp 235 trillion (25 percent of GDP). The budgetary costs of servicing the bonds and the operational costs of IBRA for 1998/99 were estimated at ½ of 1 percent of GDP in the original program. They have since been revised to about 1½ percent of GDP, reflecting higher estimates of the required support (on account of the effects of the deterioration in the economy and the depreciation of the exchange rate). However, because of delays in issuing the bonds, the cost estimate reflects interest payments for less than a full year. The full-year costs are estimated to be about 2 percent of GDP.

Korea. Public funds have been made available to purchase bad loans from commercial and merchant banks and to honor commitments under the deposit insurance scheme. Assistance has been financed mostly through issues of government-guaranteed bonds. There have also been swaps of government assets for the bank restructuring agency's claims on banks.

The total public cost of bank restructuring is currently estimated at W 75 trillion (18 percent of GDP), including W 65 trillion in government-guaranteed bonds. The interest costs to the budget in 1998 is estimated at 0.8 percent of GDP, reflecting the late start to the issuance of bonds. However, because the pace of bond issues is expected to increase, it is projected that the interest cost to the budget will rise by about 1½ to 2 percentage points of GDP over the medium term. Estimated costs are also likely to increase with the imposition of tightened prudential regulations.

Thailand. The Financial Institutions Development Fund (FIDF) provides liquidity support to finance companies and commercial banks. Plans have recently been announced to replace FIDF short-term borrowing (from the interbank market and the central bank) with longer-term government bonds. Under a note exchange program, FIDF has also made payments on promissory notes held by depositors and creditors of suspended finance companies. Apart from the operations of the FIDF, other forms of public support include central government capital contributions.

The stock of obligations incurred by the state on account of financial sector restructuring is projected to rise from B 1.4 trillion (28 percent of GDP) at end-1997/98 to B 2.1 trillion (38 percent of GDP) at end-1999/2000. On the basis of a much lower estimate of public sector support, the interest costs of the original program estimated the fiscal costs of financial sector restructuring at about 1 percent of GDP for 1997/98. During the fourth program review (August 1998), it was estimated that the interest cost of servicing the total stock of debt from all forms of financial assistance will rise from 3 percent of GDP in 1997/98 to about 4 percent in 1998/99 and 1999/2000.

References

Bascand, Geoffrey, and Assaf Razin, 1997, "Indonesia's Fiscal Position: Sustainability Issues," in *Macroeconomic Issues Facing ASEAN Countries,* ed. by John Hicklin, David Robinson, and Anoop Singh (Washington: International Monetary Fund).

Bennett, Adam, Maria Carkovic, and Louis Dicks-Mireaux, 1995, "Record of Fiscal Adjustment," in *IMF Conditionality: Experience Under Stand-By and Extended Arrangements, Part II: Background Papers,* IMF Occasional Paper No. 129 (Washington: International Monetary Fund).

Daniel, James A., Jeffrey M. Davis, and Andrew M. Wolfe, 1997, "Fiscal Accounting of Bank Restructuring," IMF Paper on Policy Analysis and Assessment No. 97/5 (Washington: International Monetary Fund).

Daniel, James, and Matthew Saal, 1997, "Macroeconomic Impact and Policy Response," in *Systematic Bank Restructuring and Macroeconomic Policy,* ed. by William E. Alexander, Jeffrey M. Davis, Liam P. Ebrill, and Carl-Johan Lindgren (Washington: International Monetary Fund).

International Monetary Fund, 1998, *World Economic Outlook, October 1998: A Survey by the Staff of the International Monetary Fund*, World Economic and Financial Surveys (Washington).

Kochhar, Kalpana, Louis Dicks-Mireaux, Balazs Horvath, Mauro Mecagni, Erik Offerdal, and Jianping Zhou, 1996, *Thailand: The Road to Sustained Growth,* IMF Occasional Paper No. 146 (Washington: International Monetary Fund).

Lane, Timothy D., 1996, "The First Round Monetary and Fiscal Impact of Bank Recapitalization in Transition Economies," IMF Paper on Policy Analysis and Assessment No. 96/8 (Washington: International Monetary Fund).

Molho, Lazaros E., 1994, "Fiscal Adjustment in an Oil-Exporting Country: The Case of Indonesia," IMF Paper on Policy Analysis and Assessment No. 94/21 (Washington: International Monetary Fund).

VIII Structural Reforms

Javier Hamann and Marianne Schulze-Ghattas

A central part of the programs in the Asian crisis countries was an unprecedented body of structural reforms ranging from restructuring insolvent financial institutions, to promoting competition in the domestic economy, to strengthening social safety nets, to addressing deficiencies in governance in financial, corporate, and government sectors. These measures were intended to address structural problems that had contributed to the crisis and to provide the foundation for a return to sustainable growth.

The World Bank and the Asian Development Bank played essential roles in developing the structural components of the programs (Box 8.1). In some instances, the initial programs mapped out areas in which more detailed plans were to be developed with the assistance of these international and regional multilateral financial organizations over the ensuing months. In Korea, for instance, these areas included corporate governance and restructuring and labor market reforms.

This section characterizes and assesses the strategy of structural reforms in these countries. It first discusses financial sector reform and corporate debt restructuring. Given the repercussions of the problems that had surfaced in these sectors, these reforms were particularly critical. The strategy pursued included both measures to handle the crisis and its aftermath and reforms to minimize the likelihood of recurrence. It inevitably evolved with events and with a deepening understanding of the problems. Some key lessons that emerge are a need to elaborate the IMF's policies in the area of financial crisis management (including the coverage of government guarantees) as well as financial and corporate restructuring; the need to treat corporate restructuring as part and parcel of financial sector restructuring; and the need to give early priority to addressing deficiencies in the institutional and legal framework for financial and corporate sector restructuring.

Reforms to enhance governance and competition, which were seen as complementing the restructuring of the financial and corporate sectors, are addressed next. This is followed by a discussion of measures to further current and capital account liberalization, which sought to prevent a lapse into beggar-my-neighbor restrictions, support competition in domestic markets, and remove the distortions that had resulted from previous partial liberalizations.

Concerns about the impact of the crisis on the poorest and most vulnerable segments of society were expressed from the outset and became increasingly pressing as the domestic recession deepened. Social sector policies are reviewed, including measures to limit unemployment, raise income transfers, and broaden social safety nets, which were regarded as an integral part of the programs.

The concluding section addresses the question of whether the structural reform agenda of the programs was too ambitious. While this question cannot entirely be dismissed—and indeed points to a need for further consideration of the appropriate pace and sequencing of reforms—the urgency of the crisis and complementarities among different reforms called for many steps to be taken simultaneously. Moreover, the programs may be viewed as providing a framework for reforms over a three-year period, including aspects to be dealt with—and spelled out in more detail—by the World Bank and the Asian Development Bank.

Financial Sector and Corporate Restructuring

Given the central role that financial sector vulnerabilities had played in bringing about the crisis, financial sector restructuring stood at the top of the structural reform agenda and formed the centerpiece of all three programs. While many previous IMF-supported programs have included measures to restructure and reform financial systems, the programs in the Asian crisis countries were unparalleled in the scope of issues that had to be dealt with under severe time constraints. There were, of course, many precedents of financial sector crises and restructuring from which to take cues, and expert knowledge was made available through extensive technical assistance from the IMF, the World Bank, and the Asian Development Bank. There was, however, no generally accepted roadmap—the structural equivalent of a financial programming framework—to guide the formulation of

Box 8.1. The World Bank and the Asian Crisis

The World Bank Group has been heavily involved in each of the three crisis countries, providing policy and technical advice, as well as financial support.

In *Korea*, the World Bank has disbursed a $3 billion Economic Reconstruction Loan (December 23, 1997) and a $2 billion Structural Adjustment Loan (March 26, 1998), in addition to technical assistance loans, and lending from the International Finance Corporation; a second, two-tranche Structural Adjustment Loan for $2 billion is planned for 1998/99. For *Thailand*, where the World Bank pledged $1.5 billion at the Tokyo meeting in August 1997, the Bank's Board approved a $15 million Financial Sector Implementation Assistance Loan (September 11, 1997) and a $350 million Finance Companies Restructuring Loan (December 23, 1997). A further Economic and Financial Adjustment Loan for $400 million, and a Social Investment Project, for $300 million, were approved in July 1998. In *Indonesia*, disbursements amounted to $899 million in 1997; in 1998, $600 million of the $1 billion Policy Reform Support Loan (approved on July 2, 1998) was disbursed, in addition to about $600 million of project-related loans.

Key areas of World Bank involvement include reform and restructuring of the financial and corporate sectors, as well as strengthening of the social safety net and reform of the labor market.

In the *financial* sector, the World Bank (in collaboration with the IMF) played an especially important role in

- Formulating and implementing the strategy for dealing with commercial banks, finance companies, and specialized financial institutions (see below).

- Assessing the solvency of the banking system and the standing of the main (systemically important) institutions, based on bank audits. The World Bank also contributed to developing plans for dealing with insolvent institutions, for disposing the assets of closed banks, and for handling the nonperforming assets of banks that were to be publicly supported.

- Improving the overall financial infrastructure, including measures to strengthen banking supervision and the redesign and reinforcement of prudential regulations in accordance with the Basle standards.

- Providing expertise on instituting (or strengthening) deposit insurance schemes.

- Updating banking laws to include provisions that had been lacking (for example, on limitations of cross ownerships between banks and enterprises).

- Strengthening the development of money markets and capital markets through the encouragement of new institutional investors (such as mutual funds), asset securitization, standardization of government bond issues, and improvement of securities market prudential rules and self-regulatory organizations (SROs).

In the *corporate* sector, the World Bank has provided technical and financial assistance for corporate restructuring (and debt restructuring) and improved corporate governance.

- In *Thailand*, the Finance Companies Restructuring Loan helped conduct in-depth assessments of the (nonsuspended) finance companies and their rehabilitation. The loan also helped strengthen prudential regulation and the supervisory regime.

- In *Indonesia*, the World Bank supported the September 1998 Jakarta Initiative's voluntary framework aimed at encouraging debtors and creditors to negotiate solutions to their debt problems on a case-by-case basis.

- In *Korea*, the Structural Adjustment and Economic Reconstruction Loans supported improvements in the responsibilities, independence, and accountability of corporate boards, and enhancement of minority shareholder and institutional investor rights; improvement in the reliability of key financial information provided by banks and corporations to regulators, shareholders, and the public; adoption by financial institutions and corporations of accounting, auditing, and reporting standards consistent with international best practices; enhancement of competition through strengthening of the Fair Trade Act; and facilitation of the liquidation of insolvent corporations.

The World Bank's efforts to improve *social safety nets* and reform *labor markets* include the following:

- In *Thailand*, a Social Investment Project intended to fund job creation through existing labor-intensive government programs; expand training for the unemployed; support low-income health insurance schemes; support small- and medium-scale community and municipal projects; and establish a monitoring system to evaluate the impact of the crisis.

- In *Indonesia*, expanded labor-intensive public works programs; actions to ensure provision of moderately priced essential goods; and initiatives to maintain access to basic education and health.

- In *Korea*, measures to increase labor market flexibility (such as elimination of restrictions on manpower leasing and strengthening employment services) while extending unemployment insurance coverage to employees of small-scale enterprises; improved poverty monitoring and protection of poverty-related public expenditures; adjustments to health insurance to improve protection of poor beneficiaries and improvements in administration; and reform of the pension system.

Source: World Bank.

the structural content of the programs from the outset. Moreover, since the programs did not anticipate the magnitude of the exchange rate depreciation and the severity of the recession (as discussed in Sections IV and V above), they likewise did not anticipate the full extent of the financial system problems that would result. In these circumstances, the strategy for financial and corporate sector restructuring was, inevitably, reactive. It evolved as initial measures proved inadequate, new information about the problems in financial institutions and corporations became available, and the difficulties themselves were aggravated by the currency depreciations and the sharp contraction of economic activity.

While the details of the reform agenda had to be worked out as the programs evolved, there was, from the outset, a consensus that the strategy had to include two broad strands: the immediate crisis, triggered by serious weaknesses in the balance sheets of financial institutions, had to be dealt with; and the systems had to be reformed to minimize the likelihood of a recurrence. Institutions that were evidently insolvent needed to be cleaned up or closed down, and a comprehensive examination of other institutions was required to assess and, if necessary, strengthen their balance sheets. These measures needed to be accompanied by steps to address the twin risks of bank runs and uncontrolled liquidity expansion. Such crisis management had to go hand in hand with credible steps to address the underlying structural weaknesses of the financial system: inadequate prudential regulation and supervision, and the legacy of a long history of direct government intervention in the allocation of credit, which had left financial institutions ill equipped to assess, price, and manage risk in an increasingly open environment. Both strands of the strategy were essential for either to succeed: strengthening weak institutions to continue business as usual in a poorly regulated system would have given at best temporary relief; by the same token, there would have been little benefit to setting adequate rules for institutions that remained in or close to insolvency.

Actions to suspend or close a number of clearly insolvent institutions were taken at (or prior to) the beginning of the programs in all three countries. While these steps were taken early to arrest further deterioration and signal the governments' resolve, they proved to be only a prelude to a long and arduous process that is still evolving. In Thailand, four months passed until a decision on the ultimate fate of the suspended finance companies was taken,[1] and a more comprehensive strategy to assess, recapitalize, and, if necessary, intervene in a broader range of financial institutions emerged only gradually in the course of the following year. In the process, a number of banks that had initially been viewed as sound turned out to be in difficulties and required intervention. In Korea, the merchant banks that were suspended at the beginning of the program were dealt with quite promptly,[2] but further interventions became necessary as the recapitalization and restructuring program was broadened to other financial institutions. In Indonesia, 16 banks, accounting for less than 3 percent of the banking sector's total deposits, were closed initially; financial sector conditions deteriorated rapidly after the initial steps amid severe political unrest and a large number of banks were intervened before a comprehensive restructuring and recapitalization plan was finally launched nearly one year after the start of the original program.[3]

All three programs emphasized the role of private funds, domestic as well as foreign, in the recapitalization and restructuring of financial institutions, but it was recognized from the outset that public money would also need to be made available, notably in connection with the resolution of suspended or closed institutions and the recapitalization of fully or partly state-owned banks. The approach that was typically followed was to request financial institutions to develop rehabilitation plans that would enable them to meet, within a specified time frame, more stringent norms regarding capital adequacy, loan classification, and provisioning. The authorities would intervene in those institutions that did not produce acceptable plans.[4]

As macroeconomic conditions deteriorated and difficulties in the financial sector spread, it became increasingly clear that the initial resolve to rely mainly on private schemes for recapitalization and restructuring was unrealistic and public funds assumed growing importance. This raised concerns about the conditionality of such funding, particularly in Korea where public funds had played a significant role from the outset,[5] and prompted efforts to define

---

[1] All but two of the 58 finance companies that had been suspended in June and August 1997 were closed in December 1997.

[2] Of the 14 merchant banks that were suspended in December 1997, 10 were closed at the end of January 1998.

[3] As of November 1998, a total of 53 banks had been brought under the auspices of the Indonesian Bank Restructuring Agency (IBRA); of these, 10 were closed.

[4] Banks that had made excessive use of central bank liquidity support were intervened (in Thailand) or placed under the auspices of IBRA (in Indonesia).

[5] Shortly after the beginning of the program, the Korean government effectively nationalized two major commercial banks through large capital injections. Significant amounts of public funds were also made available through the Korea Asset Management Corporation, which acquired nonperforming assets from financial institutions, initially with little conditionality.

more precisely the conditions under which public money would be made available, including the nature and extent of the required private contributions. As a result of the growing reliance on public funds, the government's stake in the financial sector increased significantly in the three countries, although the programs contain clear commitments regarding early reprivatization.

While the recapitalization and restructuring of a large part of the financial system is inevitably a lengthy process, shortcomings in the institutional and legal framework in the crisis countries helped to prolong it. In both Indonesia and Thailand, it took several months to establish agencies to oversee and manage the restructuring process, and more than half a year passed until procedural and legal aspects of their operations were clarified.[6] In addition, laws and regulations concerning write-downs of shareholder capital, collateral protection, privatization of state banks, and foreign ownership of financial institutions had to be reviewed and modified. The original programs generally recognized the need for action in these areas, but many specific measures were developed only as the programs evolved, and implementation of the necessary changes took considerable time, particularly in Indonesia and Thailand.[7] In retrospect, these legal and institutional changes should have been given higher priority in the early phase of the programs as they were a precondition for restructuring to proceed.

Prior to the crisis, only Korea had a formal deposit insurance system, but the general perception in all three countries was that a large part of the deposit base was covered by implicit government guarantees. This perception changed when the crisis broke. Faced with the possibility of widespread bank runs, both Korea and Thailand announced broad-based guarantees to calm depositors. The programs accepted this approach, but sought to minimize the risk of moral hazard by stressing the need for a strict time limit (and replacement by a funded and more limited deposit insurance system) as well as accompanying measures such as guarantee fees and caps

on deposit rates.[8] Indonesia initially followed a different route and promised compensation only to small depositors of the banks that were closed at the beginning of the program.[9] In addition to the limited coverage for deposits in private banks, the guarantee was not widely publicized, and no announcement was made regarding the treatment of depositors in other institutions that had not yet been intervened. After several waves of deposit runs, a comprehensive guarantee scheme covering all bank depositors and creditors for a period of two years was introduced in January 1998.

While bank runs were particularly severe in Indonesia, they also occurred in the initial phases of the programs in Korea and Thailand. In response, central banks stepped up liquidity support for the affected institutions. In principle, this support was to be short term and subject to conditions. In practice, notably in Indonesia and Thailand, the funds were repeatedly rolled over and intervention of the institutions that relied heavily on this financing eventually became necessary. Conditionality was typically limited to punitive interest rates, which were, however, not much of a deterrent for institutions that were already insolvent, especially as in many instances the interest was capitalized. Moreover, in Korea, the interest spreads charged on the central bank's foreign currency support for banks soon lagged behind soaring market spreads and had to be adjusted significantly to discourage extensive use of the facility. While in Korea and Thailand, liquidity support by the central bank[10] was relatively quickly sterilized and brought under control, in Indonesia it helped to derail the monetary program and eventually necessitated a fundamental overhaul of Bank Indonesia's liquidity facilities.[11]

The programs recognized from the outset that fundamental improvements in the regulatory and supervisory framework in the crisis countries would be required to ensure that financial institutions would start operating on a sound basis. Without such measures to address the "flow problem," efforts to deal with weak balance sheets (the "stock problem") would at best enjoy temporary success. In the initial phase, the pro-

---

[6]In Indonesia, IBRA was established in February 1998, but amendments to the banking act endowing it with legal power were passed by Parliament only in October. Moreover, there are doubts that these amendments are fully adequate for the efficient functioning of IBRA. In Thailand, the Financial Restructuring Agency (FRA) lacked for months the legal power to restructure the loans of the intervened financial institutions, thus delaying corporate restructuring.

[7]In Thailand, for example, major initiatives such as a revision of the bankruptcy law and an emergency decree to facilitate bank mergers were still on the agenda more than one year after the beginning of the program. In Indonesia, legislation eliminating restrictions on foreign investment in banks and enabling mergers and privatization of state banks was passed only in October 1998.

[8]These caps were formulated with reference to the rates offered by the strongest banks and were intended to prevent weak banks from bidding up deposit rates.

[9]The guarantee referred to deposits up to the equivalent of about $5,000, covering over 90 percent of depositors but only 20 percent of the deposit base of the closed institutions. [10]In Thailand, the agency that formally acts as lender of last resort is the Financial Institutions Development Fund, which operates under the auspices of the Bank of Thailand.

[10]In Thailand, the agency that formally acts as lender of last resort is the Financial Institutions Development Fund, which operates under the auspices of the Bank of Thailand.

[11]Section VI above discusses the role of banking system problems in derailing Indonesia's monetary program.

grams typically focused on incremental improvements in loan classification and provisioning standards, capital adequacy requirements, and foreign exchange exposure limits. In view of the precarious situation of many financial institutions, a degree of regulatory forbearance was generally accepted and more stringent requirements were typically introduced in a graduated fashion. However, the tightening of loan classification standards frequently lagged behind the tightening of capital adequacy requirements, rendering the latter less meaningful.

Comprehensive revisions of prudential regulations are under way in all three countries. The ultimate objective of these reforms is to bring regulatory standards in line with Basle Core Principles and, particularly in Korea, to expand their coverage to institutions that were previously not subject to these requirements.[12] In addition to loan classification and capital adequacy standards, the planned revisions cover restrictions on foreign exchange and liquidity exposure as well as rules regarding lending to connected parties. Steps have also been taken to improve accounting standards and tighten disclosure requirements for financial institutions.

As the process of financial sector restructuring advanced, the importance of complementary measures to address weaknesses in the corporate sector became increasingly evident. In Korea and Indonesia, deficiencies in corporate governance were recognized at the outset, but were not given high priority.[13] In Korea's initial program, corporate governance and restructuring was one of the areas in which the World Bank was to assist in devising detailed plans, but a plan to encourage corporate financial restructuring was to be formulated only by late 1998. The urgency of corporate restructuring was recognized only at a later stage when problems in the financial system spread in the wake of the deepening domestic recession. In order to deal with the growing corporate debt problem, frameworks were developed for voluntary debt workouts between bank creditors and corporate debtors, and in some cases public financial contributions to the recapitalization of financial institutions were made conditional on progress with corporate debt workouts.[14]

In Indonesia, where the corporate sector accounted for the lion's share of external debt, the special problems of external corporate debt had to be addressed in talks with foreign bank creditors. These talks led to the establishment of a government exchange guarantee scheme—the INDRA scheme—which was subsequently complemented by a set of nonbinding guidelines for debt workouts with domestic and foreign creditors (the Jakarta Initiative), but progress with corporate debt restructuring has, so far, been very slow.[15] Similar guidelines were formulated in Thailand by the newly established Corporate Debt Restructuring Advisory Committee, and in Korea, financial institutions committed themselves to a binding framework by signing a Corporate Restructuring Agreement that involves arbitration.

The frameworks for corporate debt workouts in all three countries are, in essence, based on the "London Approach," which describes a set of principles under which creditors agree to keep credit facilities in place, seek out-of-court solutions, work together, share all relevant information about the debtor, and recognize the seniority of claims.[16] In addition, the three program countries have implemented or initiated a number of legal and regulatory reforms to facilitate corporate restructuring and enhance corporate governance, ranging from the elimination of cross guarantees in conglomerates in Korea to changes in prudential regulations regarding the treatment of restructured debt in Thailand. These legal reforms, in particular in the area of bankruptcy legislation, are an essential precondition for corporate debt restructuring to proceed. In the absence of the credible threat of foreclosure and bankruptcy procedures that define the rights of creditors and debtors, voluntary debt restructuring was unlikely to progress very far.[17]

The reform agenda for the financial and corporate sectors in the crisis countries is still evolving and it is too early for a detailed assessment of the multitude of measures that were planned and implemented. Nevertheless, the experience with financial and corporate sector restructuring during the first program year raises a number of important general questions regarding program design that can be addressed at this stage.

---

[12]In Korea, the supervision of bank and nonbank financial institutions was unified at the beginning of the program, but different standards continued to apply to different types of institutions.

[13]In Korea, attention focused on the lack of transparency and the high debt-equity ratios of large conglomerates (*chaebol*); in Indonesia, concerns centered on the state enterprises and numerous regulatory impediments to competition. The latter are discussed in the next section.

[14]The recapitalization program announced in August 1998 in Thailand contains this type of conditionality.

[15]Under this scheme, the Indonesia Debt Restructuring Agency (INDRA) acts as an intermediary between the domestic debtor and the foreign creditor in the servicing of renegotiated foreign debt. Debt-service payments are made to INDRA in domestic currency on the basis of a specified exchange rate, which is guaranteed in real terms. INDRA does not take on commercial risk and is not involved in actual debt workouts, which are to be guided by the principles outlined under the Jakarta Initiative.

[16]The London Approach is used to guide voluntary debt restructuring in the United Kingdom.

[17]Bankruptcy laws were strengthened relatively early in Korea (February 1998) and Indonesia (April 1998), but much later in Thailand (October 1998).

The overriding question is whether it was appropriate to place so much emphasis on structural measures in the financial and corporate sectors, which, at least in the initial phase, had to be developed under severe time constraints. The answer is clearly yes. Given the state of the financial system and the related difficulties in the corporate sector, which played a key role in the emergence of the crisis, the programs would have had little chance of success and little hope of gaining credibility without beginning a set of decisive steps to address these problems. Macroeconomic policies would have been undermined by the continuing deterioration of financial sector conditions, which was bound to lead to rapid liquidity expansion and a ballooning of quasi-fiscal deficits. Moreover, the ultimate goal of the programs—a quick return to sustainable growth—would not have been possible in an environment of protracted and deepening structural problems in the financial and corporate sectors.

Another important question is whether it would have been preferable to take more time to develop a comprehensive and detailed strategy—a precise roadmap—for the structural content of the programs rather than embarking without delay on a road for which only the broad outlines and some details of the first few miles were known at the outset. Given the nature of the crisis—a vicious circle of growing problems in the financial sector and a worsening macroeconomic environment—there was no alternative to the predominantly reactive approach that characterized policies in all three countries. Failure to begin to address the weaknesses of financial institutions early on would have implied a continuing rapid deterioration of financial sector conditions with attendant macroeconomic consequences; this likely would have deepened the crisis.

A number of lessons can be drawn from the experience with financial and corporate sector restructuring in the Asian crisis countries, lessons that should help streamline crisis management in the future. For one, the experience suggests that it would be highly desirable for the IMF and the World Bank to formulate policy guidelines on the key issues that need to be dealt with in the context of a financial sector crisis.[18] For example, the experience with bank closures and subsequent bank runs in Indonesia raises questions about the initial policy on government guarantees: why did it differ fundamentally from the policy adopted in the two other program countries, even though (given widespread knowledge that the closed banks represented only a subset of a much larger number of insolvent institutions) the risk of bank runs in Indonesia was considerably higher? The policy was reversed two months later, but the problems encountered as a result of the initial approach contributed (along with other factors) to throwing the program off track.

Another important lesson from the experience in the Asian crisis is that measures to address deficiencies in the institutional and legal framework for financial sector restructuring need to be given high priority at the beginning of the process to avoid unnecessary delays. In addition, it needs to be recognized that corporate restructuring is a necessary complement to financial sector restructuring and frameworks for corporate debt workouts, as well as related reforms in bankruptcy laws and other relevant legislation, need to be introduced at an early stage.

An understanding on the need for early action in these areas, together with policy guidelines on key issues such as guarantees, the extent and form of regulatory forbearance, or the conditionality of liquidity support for distressed institutions, would help streamline the restructuring process and inform decisions on a variety of structural issues that have to be made in the midst of a crisis. At the same time, it must be recognized that, given the complexity of the issues involved and country-specific conditions that need to be taken into account, no amount of institutional wisdom will suffice to produce a straightforward template for policies.

Financial and corporate sector restructuring tends to be a protracted process even under favorable circumstances. During this process, uncertainty about the state of the financial system and the corporate sector is likely to persist for some time and to influence market perceptions of private sector creditworthiness. Thus, there may have been an undue degree of optimism in the implicit assumption that market confidence would be significantly boosted in the short run by the combined policy and financing packages in the original Asian crisis programs.

Governance and Competition Policy

Reforms intended to improve governance and promote competition were a prominent aspect of the programs in the Asian crisis countries. It was recognized that the vulnerabilities in the financial and corporate sectors in these countries were attributable, in part, to deficiencies that undermined governance and market discipline: notably, the lack of well-defined and transparent accounting and regulatory standards, inadequate disclosure requirements, and complex formal and informal ties between government, financial institutions, and corporations.

---

[18]Indeed, this has already begun under the Financial Sector Liaison Committee established by the two institutions.

Reforms to promote governance and competition in the program countries included dismantling state-sponsored monopolies and cartels; privatizing state enterprises that had served as vehicles of "crony capitalism"; strengthening competition laws; improving corporate disclosure requirements and increasing accountability to shareholders; increasing the transparency of economic and financial data; and restructuring or dismantling corporate networks (such as *chaebol* in Korea) that had limited the transparency of intercorporate dealings. To ensure that state enterprises were not merely sold into the hands of political insiders, competitive bidding procedures for privatization were established. Competitive bidding was introduced for government procurement as well. In addition, tax and regulatory structures that had led to distortions and misallocations of resources, including by bolstering monopolies, were reformed.

In Indonesia, efforts to improve governance and competition included a broad range of reforms ranging from the elimination of various types of formal and informal restrictive marketing arrangements to measures to enhance governance in state enterprises and prepare them for privatization. Box 8.2 illustrates the scope of these reforms. In Korea, policies focused in particular on strengthening shareholders' rights; eliminating government interference with bankruptcy procedures, mergers, and acquisitions; and enhancing the transparency of the business practices of conglomerates, including through restrictions on cross guarantees. In Thailand, the main emphasis has been on privatization. Preliminary work for the privatization of (and share divestiture from) public enterprises in the areas of energy, utilities, communications, and transport has been completed; a privatization secretariat has been established; and legislative measures needed to facilitate privatization of "noncorporatized" public enterprises have been proposed. In addition, work on the development of an adequate regulatory framework has been initiated.

In order to increase transparency in the public and private sectors, the programs included a number of measures to improve the quality, frequency, and timeliness of economic and financial data. These measures focused in particular on international reserves, foreign liabilities, and indicators of financial sector conditions, such as nonperforming loans and capital adequacy ratios. In addition, steps were taken to publish information on ownership structures and affiliations of financial institutions, and improve corporate accounting standards with a view to bringing them in line with internationally accepted practices. Efforts were also strengthened to ensure compliance by the end of 1998 with the IMF's Special Data Dissemination Standard to which the countries had earlier subscribed.

Current and Capital Account Liberalization

The programs in Indonesia and Korea included a number of measures to further liberalize external trade. The strategy typically focused on the continuation or acceleration of existing liberalization plans to prevent a lapse into beggar-my-neighbor restrictions—a tempting alternative at a time of crisis. In addition, trade liberalization measures were intended to support other measures aimed at promoting domestic competition. Indonesia accelerated the implementation of a comprehensive program introduced in 1995 to decrease most tariffs, reduce the number of products subject to special trade regimes, and gradually eliminate most nontariff barriers. Korea is planning to set a timetable for the elimination of trade-related subsidies, restrictive import licensing, and the import diversification program.[19] Measures were also adopted to increase the transparency of import certification procedures.

Capital account liberalization was one of the more controversial structural policies in the programs, especially in Korea, given that excessive exposure to capital movements was viewed as one of the factors leading to the crisis. The crisis countries had taken important steps to liberalize their capital accounts prior to the crisis, and the IMF had generally encouraged such steps.[20] However, in Korea, the way in which liberalization had been approached had contributed to its vulnerability. In particular, the experience of the crisis underscored the importance of appropriate sequencing to avoid creating distortions through selective liberalization of different types of flows, and the need for adequate standards of prudential supervision and regulation for institutions that have access to international capital markets.[21] For example, the partial nature of the liberalization in Korea had encouraged short-term international borrowing by domestic financial institutions for on-lending to the corporate sector. Given the long-term efficiency benefits of capital account liberalization and the difficulty of reversing the process once it has started, the decision was made to move forward and remove the existing distortions through more comprehensive liberalization. Korea is speeding up its ongoing capital account liberalization program, including by eliminating restrictions on long-term foreign borrowing by corporations, pacing this with im-

---

[19]Korea's import diversification program requires importers to limit imports from countries that run a large bilateral trade surplus vis-à-vis Korea.

[20]In Indonesia the capital account had been liberalized well before the crisis; the "free foreign exchange system" had been a pillar of economic policy for the past 30 years.

[21]See, for instance, Johnston and others (1997).

Box 8.2. Indonesia: Improving Governance and Competition

Notwithstanding steps to liberalize Indonesia's economy over the previous decade, at the time of the crisis there remained considerable limits on competition: in addition to barriers to foreign trade and investment, extensive domestic regulation restricted competition and supported monopolies or cartels in important sectors. A number of these restrictions intersected with governance issues, which added to perceptions of inequity and creating uncertainty for both domestic and foreign investors. Indeed, structural impediments to economic activity were seen as central to market concerns about Indonesia's future prospects.

Indonesia's program reflected these concerns, featuring not only measures to further liberalize foreign trade and investment but also domestic deregulation. An ambitious structural policy program prepared in cooperation with the World Bank therefore called for a number of fundamental changes:

- An end to agricultural import and domestic marketing monopolies and price controls, including the abolition of the monopoly of the state trading agency (BULOG) over the importation and distribution of essential food items. More generally, elimination of all formal and informal restrictive marketing arrangements.

- In both retail and wholesale trade, elimination of restrictions on foreign investment.

- Prohibiting provincial governments from restricting trade within Indonesia, and the elimination of provincial and local export taxes.

- Release of farmers from requirements for the forced planting of sugar cane.

- Measures to allow private participation in the provision of public infrastructure, with transparent and competitive bidding.

- International standard audits of several large state enterprises.

- Preparation of a law on competition.

Establishment of a competitive environment also requires procedures for the orderly exit of nonviable firms. Facilitating this were improvements in bankruptcy law and the establishment of a corporate debt restructuring scheme.

Competition and governance were also to be improved by measures relating to the management and privatization of state enterprises. Among these were

- Restructuring of state-owned enterprises, as a prelude to accelerated privatization.

- Steps to sharply define responsibility and accountability for managing firms in the public sector.

- Establishment of transparent procedures for divestiture and privatization.

Early in Indonesia's program, implementation of structural policies generally was very uneven; indeed, the authorities took a number of steps backward, especially in areas involving governance. A particular problem area was in exposing BULOG to effective competition—as, for instance, certain new subsidies were extended only to BULOG; in response, the program prescribed measures to level the playing field by offering the subsidies also to BULOG's competitors. (However, some discrimination in favor of BULOG remained.)

In general, as the program continued there was considerable progress in promoting competition, despite the inevitable resistance to dismantling policies that generate monopoly rents to be distributed to political insiders. Corresponding to these lost rents, of course, are gains to consumers and probably a more equitable distribution of income.

---

provements in the supervision and regulation of the domestic financial sector.

Social Sector Policies

Concerns about the effects of the crisis on the most vulnerable segments of society played a significant role in the programs from the outset, given the rudimentary formal social safety nets in the three countries.[22] These concerns became more pressing, however, as it became clear that the downturn in economic activity would be much harsher than initially expected. This prompted a series of additional measures to alleviate the impact of price increases and rising unemployment on the poor.[23]

---

[22]Existing social safety nets in the three countries are described in Gupta and others (1998). They typically include some form of insurance for old age, disability, and death with very limited coverage and benefits; rudimentary health insurance and insurance for work-related injuries; and, in Indonesia and Korea, limited social assistance programs for poor persons without income and for particularly vulnerable groups. Of the three program countries, only Korea had a formal unemployment insurance system, which covered, however, only a small portion of the labor force at the onset of the crisis.

[23]While it is difficult to estimate the impact of rising prices and unemployment on the incidence of poverty, staff calculations based on the *World Economic Outlook* suggest that the number of poor in Indonesia could increase by 5 to 11 percentage points of the population, in Korea by 2 to 12 percentage points, and in Thailand by 3 to 12 percentage points (see International Monetary Fund, 1998).

Box 8.3. Social Sector Policies in Indonesia, Korea, and Thailand[1]

Indonesia

Given the sharp contraction of economic activity and steep price increases due to currency depreciation, a severe drought, and the disruption of supply channels in the wake of political unrest, social sector policies have focused on the availability of key commodities and basic services at subsidized prices, and on limiting unemployment.

Subsidies for food and other essential goods and services. While across-the-board subsidies are to be phased out, the program allowed for substantial increases in subsidies on essential foodstuffs such as rice, soybeans, sugar, wheat flour, corn, soybean meal, and fishmeal to stabilize prices. Subsidies on these products, except rice, had been eliminated (as they were found to benefit only traders, not consumers), but all fuel and electricity prices as well as low-cost housing continue to be highly subsidized; it is these subsidies that comprise the bulk of safety net spending. In addition, steps have been taken to rehabilitate the distribution system.

Health care and education. To support the provision of health care to the poor, a new subsidy scheme for essential drugs for rural and urban health centers has been introduced, and budgetary allocations for various health care projects have been increased. Measures to support education include a new scholarship program, grants to replace existing school fees, and an expansion of school lunch programs.

Employment generating projects. Community-based public works programs have been introduced in rural and urban areas, and special credit schemes for small enterprises have been expanded.

Korea

While still rudimentary by the standards of member countries of the Organization for Economic Cooperation and Development (OECD), Korea's social safety net is more developed than the corresponding systems in Indonesia and Thailand, which lack formal unemployment insurance schemes. Inflation has been kept in check, but unemployment has risen sharply as economic activity has contracted and existing restrictions on layoffs have been eased. To balance measures to increase labor market flexibility, social sector policies under the program have focused mainly on strengthening the unemployment insurance system, bringing it closer into line with other OECD countries.

Expansion of the unemployment insurance scheme. Coverage of the system has been broadened in steps

from firms with more than 30 employees prior to the program to firms with more than 5 employees; the scheme now covers 70 percent of the labor force. In addition, the minimum level of benefits has been raised and the minimum duration of benefits has been increased. Eligibility for benefits has been expanded temporarily by reducing the minimum contribution period and raising the maximum duration of benefits.

Measures to support employment and training. Several programs have been introduced to encourage firms to resort to reduced hours and training instead of layoffs, and training allowances provided under the employment insurance system have been increased. Public works programs have also been used to support employment.

Income transfers to the poor. Budgetary allocations for social welfare assistance, including support for persons without income, have been raised significantly.

Thailand

While inflation has been kept under control, the sharp contraction in output and the associated increase in unemployment since the onset of the crisis has exposed the weaknesses of Thailand's very limited formal social safety net. Social sector policies, supported by the Asian Development Bank, the World Bank, and the Overseas Economic Cooperation Fund, have relied on a broad range of measures to mitigate the impact of the crisis on the poor.

Employment generating projects. Temporary civil works programs in construction and infrastructure rehabilitation have been initiated. In addition, two funds to support employment-creating investment projects in rural communities and municipalities are being established, and a program to promote rural industrial employment is being expanded.

Support for the unemployed. The severance pay provided by employers to dismissed employees has been increased to 10 months (for workers with more than 10 years of service), and an assistance fund to provide cash support to laid-off workers of bankrupt firms has been established. Eligibility for benefits under the limited social security system (medical, disability, and death) has been extended to the unemployed for up to 12 months. In addition, training programs and job placement facilities are being expanded.

Health and education. To support access to health care by the poor, financial support for community-based health care projects, particularly in rural areas, is being increased, and the public health insurance scheme for low-income groups is being strengthened. To preserve education standards, scholarship and loan programs are being expanded, and spending in key areas has been protected.

Price subsidies. Urban bus and rail transportation continues to be provided at subsidized fares.

---

[1]The summary of social sector policies in this box refers to the programs as of mid-1998 (following the third review). Given initial expectations that the impact of the crisis on output and employment would be much less severe, the scope of social sector policies in the original programs was typically more limited.

Many of these measures, particularly in Thailand, were designed and financed with support from the Asian Development Bank and the World Bank. In addition, efforts were made to involve the affected parties in the development of social sector policies. In Korea, for example, reforms affecting the labor market and unemployment compensation were based on a Tripartite Agreement between the government, employer organizations, and trade unions.

While the focus of social sector policies in the three countries has varied, the programs typically included measures in four broad areas: measures to raise income transfers by strengthening and broadening the scope of existing social safety nets; measures to limit unemployment through government support for various types of employment and training schemes, as well as self-employment initiatives; measures to limit the impact of price increases on the consumption of poor households through new support schemes or the continuation of existing subsidies for basic goods and services, such as food, energy, and transportation; and measures to maintain access by the poor to health care and education (Box 8.3).[24] In designing social sector policies, the programs sought to target assistance to protect the vulnerable while avoiding labor market disincentives and an unsustainable burden for the budget. Nevertheless, given the severity of the recession, significant increases in budgetary outlays for social programs were adopted, ranging from 2 percent of GDP in Korea to about 6 percent of GDP in Indonesia in 1998.

General Observations

Critics of the programs in the Asian crisis countries have argued that they suffered from an "overload" of structural reforms. Given the large and steadily widening structural reform agenda that had to be dealt with, this criticism cannot be dismissed lightly.[25]

---

[24]The different types of measures are summarized in Gupta and others (1998).

[25]At the same time, the perception of overload may have been exaggerated by the fact that in several areas (such as corporate-governance and labor market reform) the intended reforms were

While it is generally accepted that something had to be done to address the problems in the financial sector, measures to enhance governance and competition, liberalize trade and capital flows, and strengthen the social safety net have been seen as less central to the logic of the programs. However, while financial and corporate sector restructuring formed the core of the structural reform agenda in all three programs, supporting reforms in other areas played an important role. They were seen as needed to remove impediments to the efficient functioning of financial, goods, and labor markets, and to cushion the social impact of the crisis. As such, they were seen as important for the sustainability of the adjustment effort and an eventual return to sustainable growth. Important questions remain, however, regarding the appropriate pace and sequencing of reforms, and the emphasis on different areas of reform—as exemplified by the fact that, over time, the programs have tended to become more sharply focused on the core of financial and corporate restructuring.

References

Gupta, S., C. McDonald, C. Schiller, M. Verhoeven, Ž. Bogetić, and G. Schwartz, 1998, "Mitigating the Social Costs of the Economic Crisis and the Reform Programs in Asia," IMF Paper on Policy Analysis and Assessment No. 98/7 (Washington: International Monetary Fund).

International Monetary Fund, 1998, *World Economic Outlook, October 1998: A Survey by the Staff of the International Monetary Fund,* World Economic and Financial Surveys (Washington).

Johnston, R. Barry, Salim M. Derber, and Claudia Echeverria, 1997, "Sequencing Capital Account Liberalization: Lessons from the Experiences in Chile, Indonesia, Korea, and Thailand," IMF Working Paper No. 97/157 (Washington: International Monetary Fund).

---

to be planned with the assistance of the World Bank and the Asian Development Bank for implementation during the three-year period of the programs and beyond.

IX   Taking Stock

Timothy Lane

This paper has presented a preliminary assessment of some key aspects of the programs in Asian crisis countries. Clearly, any conclusions drawn at this stage, while events are still unfolding, must necessarily be tentative. Moreover, the experiences of the countries examined contain many important differences as well as similarities. It is nonetheless useful to try to distill some lessons from the experience so far.

The programs adopted by the authorities and endorsed by the IMF were based on the assumption that policies, together with the commitment of official financing, would restore confidence in the markets and attract private capital flows; official financing and current account adjustment would then need to be sufficient to satisfy the external financing constraint. The more successful the strategy in restoring confidence, the more limited would be the need for disbursement of the official commitment of funds. However, in the event, particularly in Indonesia, but also in Thailand and in Korea, the programs and their initial implementation did not restore confidence rapidly enough, capital accounts were much less favorable than assumed and so the reverse happened: given the climate of economic and political uncertainty, investors (including domestic ones) were not reassured, so a vicious circle of capital outflows and depreciation resulted. The vicious circle was exacerbated as deepening insolvency of financial institutions and corporations created counterparty risk that added to pressure on the foreign exchange market. The depreciations and the severe recessions that ensued took most of the burden of closing the financing gap through a massive current account adjustment. More recently, markets have been stabilized with the restoration of confidence, and exchange rates have appreciated toward precrisis levels.

The expenditure-switching effect of exchange rate depreciation in these economies was attenuated by the concurrent depreciations in several countries in the region. At the same time, the depreciations had strong expenditure-reducing effects via their impact on the balance sheets of financial institutions and corporations. Further balance sheet effects came from sharp drops in asset prices and the disclosure of existing problems in portfolio quality. The resulting wealth effects and disruptions to financing, along with adverse effects on confidence, were reflected in a collapse of domestic investment and a severe decline in consumption associated with the sharp economic downturn. The downturn was also exacerbated by other shocks: internal economic and social disruption (whose seriousness differed across countries) had adverse effects on aggregate supply, while external demand was further weakened by other factors such as the deepening slump in Japan. However, the magnitude of the downturn was largely forced on these economies by the substantial current account adjustment dictated by capital outflows for which it was impossible to compensate through even larger official financing.

The program projections badly misgauged the severity of the downturn. In part, this reflected the fact that the IMF's projections were somewhat more sanguine than the consensus, partly reflecting pressures to agree with the authorities on a common set of program projections and, perhaps, partly a concern to avoid damaging confidence through gloomy forecasts. Erring on the side of optimism in this way was probably detrimental to the programs' credibility. However, it should also be noted that very few foresaw the severity of the downturn—neither the authorities, the private sector, nor academic observers. Failing to foresee the depth of the recession meant that the monetary programs were originally set to allow more rapid growth of money and credit; and fiscal targets were originally more restrictive than they would otherwise have been;[1] it also meant underestimating the magnitude of financial sector restructuring needed.

A variety of factors conspired to make it more difficult to restore confidence. These factors included political uncertainties, the appearance of irresolution in policies, difficulties in communicating the logic

---

[1]At the same time, since higher projected growth implies higher projected revenues, the fiscal measures estimated to be consistent with reaching given targets for the fiscal balance would be *less* stringent.

and features of the programs to the markets and the public, problems in the coverage of government guarantees, some lack of public support for the programs, and the public debate that took place regarding certain aspects of the IMF-supported programs. Moreover, these factors were operating in a setting where programs were vulnerable to such shifts in market sentiments: the programs' financing had been based on the assumption of a high rollover rate for private short-term debt—in effect, assuming that a virtuous circle would materialize. The phased, contingent nature of official commitments, and uncertainty over the disbursement of the second lines of defense, may also have been factors weakening efforts to restore confidence.

It is thus clear, in hindsight, that the programs were not adequately financed to be carried out in an environment where the crucial effort to restore confidence failed. There would have been two obvious hypothetical alternatives: more official financing or greater private sector bail-in. More official financing would have been difficult, given limited resources and moral hazard considerations. Earlier concerted involvement of the private sector could have been pursued, but if done too aggressively there could have been adverse consequences for emerging markets more generally if the private sector concluded that there had been a change in the rules of the game. Here, the main lesson is that such avenues should be explored in preparation for the next crisis; that is, instruments and mechanisms need to be found to elicit the maintenance of private sector exposure to a country facing a potential loss of market access, without inducing adverse contagion.

The decision to float exchange rates—in the absence of any clear domestic policy anchor to focus expectations—opened the door to continued market depreciation. But there was no practical alternative under the IMF-supported programs, especially in Thailand and Korea where the initial efforts of the authorities to defend their exchange rates resulted in the exhaustion of reserves and removed much of their room for maneuver. Credible step devaluations may have been possible and less disruptive, but only when the countries still had resources and the resolve to defend a new peg. If rates had been repegged based on expectations of capital flows at the time of the programs, they would soon have had to give way in the face of the capital outflows, unless a punishingly tight interest rate policy had been attempted—and that with no guarantee of success.

Although no targets were announced for exchange rates, the exchange rate was the central focus of monetary policy, and interest rates the operating target. The monetary performance criteria specified in the programs were not so much policy targets as secondary tools for monitoring policy outcomes. Policy

itself concentrated on leaning against the wind with regard to exchange rate movements. This approach—which put the emphasis on adapting policy to changing conditions—may have been the only viable option in the crisis. The exchange rate was the best available guide to policy, as no other nominal variable was immediately observable.

The basic objective of monetary policy in these programs was to avoid an inflation-depreciation spiral. As suggested by the experience of Indonesia, the possibility of such a spiral was genuine, even in countries with a track record of relatively low inflation. Given concern that excessive monetary tightening could severely depress economic activity, though, the policy followed in the programs was intended as a middle course, leaning against the wind in the foreign exchange market rather than an all-out pursuit of any exchange rate target.

During 1997, the authorities in all three program countries showed some reluctance to tighten monetary policies, both before and after exchange rate pegs were abandoned. This initial vacillation made the task of stabilizing more difficult later on. By early 1998, nevertheless, significant tightening had occurred in Korea and Thailand, but this tightening was not extreme when set against the benchmark of previous crises elsewhere, and is unlikely to have been a major factor behind the output decline. At the same time, persistent reports of credit crunches are of concern. These may be attributable largely to dislocations in the microeconomic allocation of credit, attributable to problems of credit risk rather than tightening of aggregate liquidity, and pointing to the need to move ahead with financial and corporate restructuring.

In Korea and Thailand, the authorities were able to ride the hurricane, and have succeeded in averting an inflation-depreciation spiral. In Indonesia, in contrast, monetary policy went widely off track and inflation became a serious concern, reflecting deeper structural as well as political and social problems and the weakness of the central bank. More recently, the situation in Indonesia has stabilized, with a substantial recovery of the rupiah.

Given unhedged foreign currency exposures, currency depreciation might have had a greater impact on corporations than the higher interest rates needed to stop it—although both are likely to have hurt, particularly given the high leverage ratios of corporations in these countries. Although monetary tightening, if carried to extremes, could in principle result in depreciation rather than appreciation, there is no evidence that this perverse response occurred in these countries.

The original programs in all three countries included some element of fiscal adjustment, in the face of an expected deterioration due to the economic environment, to make room for part of the prospective costs of bank restructuring and to support the external adjustment and thus bolster confidence. The fiscal measures presented in the initial programs were fairly modest in Korea and Indonesia (and even smaller when compared with the expected outcome for the previous fiscal year rather than to the authorities' original plans for the program period). In Thailand, where initial fiscal and external current account imbalances were larger, the fiscal measures in the initial program were more substantial.

Fiscal plans were revised substantially during the course of the programs in response to changing economic conditions—specifically, declining economic activity, a deteriorating external environment, unduly depreciated exchange rates, and (in Indonesia) falling oil prices. In the early program reviews, additional measures were introduced to offset part of the deterioration of the fiscal balance resulting from changing conditions. More recently, with growing concerns over the recession throughout the region, and lesser need for external adjustment due to the rapid adjustment in the current account, the balance of priorities has shifted toward supporting output and increasing the support available under social safety nets. From an early stage, fiscal deficits were allowed to expand to accommodate at least part of the automatic effect of declining activity and income and the exchange rate depreciations, providing support for economic activity from early 1998 on. In recent reviews, fiscal programs have been eased further to augment the automatic stabilizers.

The overall direction of fiscal policy measures can be seen by examining how the change in the fiscal balance was affected by policy changes. By this measure, fiscal policy actions are estimated to have significantly expansionary effects in both Korea and Thailand, relative to a policy of pure accommodation. In Indonesia, in contrast, fiscal policy changes offset up to one-third of the very large deterioration in the fiscal balance associated with changing economic conditions (where the latter includes the increase in food subsidies in response to the exchange rate depreciation). These results do not give credence to the view that fiscal stringency was a major factor accounting for the output decline in these countries.

Given the need for external adjustment forced by the capital outflows during the crisis, fiscal policy may have had more influence on the composition than on the magnitude of the output decline. An easier fiscal policy at the outset would likely have required more real exchange rate adjustment and/or higher interest rates in the face of capital outflows, depressing private domestic expenditure further via balance sheet effects. The net stimulus to economic activity might thus have been relatively small. By the same token, the recent shift of policies in the direction of supporting activity has become appropriate in light of the external adjustment by the private sector, and the easing of the external financing constraint with the abating crisis.

Although a complete understanding of these countries' structural problems emerged only as events unfolded, it was known from the start that structural reforms needed to be a central pillar of the programs. A strong package of structural reforms was essential, in light of major weaknesses, especially in the financial and corporate sectors, that underlay the crisis. Critics have argued that since many reforms, even if sensible in the medium term, have some adjustment costs, the large number of reforms entailed an excessive burden at a time of great economic weakness. While these concerns cannot be dismissed lightly, they ignore the real nature of the crisis—much more the result of cumulating structural weaknesses than of macroeconomic maladjustment. In that context, lasting recovery depended on comprehensive structural change. Attempting stabilization without strong structural reforms, especially in the financial and corporate sectors, would have been a costly effort to treat the symptoms without credibly addressing the causes of the disease. Moreover, in light of complementarities among different reform measures, dropping some of the reform measures from the packages on the grounds that they were too costly or too difficult to put in place would likely have impaired the effectiveness of others. Indeed, as the programs evolved, they revealed greater depths and complexities to the weaknesses that the reforms were to address. At this point, however, hindsight suggests that corporate restructuring should have been given higher priority at the outset—as indeed it was given increasing emphasis as the programs evolved.

Critics have also argued that closures of financial institutions at the outset of the programs undermined confidence (especially in Indonesia) and that any needed closures should have been delayed. However, delays in closures may only have made their costs larger. The main problem with Indonesia's banks during November 1997–January 1998 was not early closure but closing a subset of problem institutions under inappropriate conditions. One factor accelerating bank runs was the initial treatment of deposit guarantees, which were very limited in amount, inadequately publicized, and covered only those institutions already closed. In contrast, the experience with financial restructuring in Korea and Thailand was much more favorable.

The record of implementation of policies shows that two of the countries—Korea and Thailand—have, on the whole, been rather successful in implementing the programs as agreed, whereas in Indonesia, in part because of the severity of the underlying political crisis, the program has repeatedly veered off course and has required substantial modification. While this period has been very difficult for all three countries, developments have been much more favorable in the two that have been able to keep to their programs. In Korea and Thailand, the challenge is to persevere with their adjustment, and get through the difficult phase where measures have begun to bite but their credibility has not yet been established, into the phase where they can start to reap the benefits. Indonesia, in contrast, still faces a more difficult task, owing to the need to repair repeated policy slippages and arrest a slide into an increasingly difficult social situation; its progress in this direction, however, has been encouraging.

Recent Occasional Papers of the International Monetary Fund

178. IMF-Supported Programs in Indonesia, Korea, and Thailand: A Preliminary Assessment, by Timothy Lane, Atish Ghosh, Javier Hamann, Steven Phillips, Marianne Schulze-Ghattas, and Tsidi Tsikata. 1999.

177. Perspectives on Regional Unemployment in Europe, by Paolo Mauro, Eswar Prasad, and Antonio Spilimbergo. 1999.

176. Back to the Future: Postwar Reconstruction and Stabilization in Lebanon, edited by Sena Eken and Thomas Helbling. 1999.

175. Macroeconomic Developments in the Baltics, Russia, and Other Countries of the Former Soviet Union, 1992–97, by Luis M. Valdivieso. 1998.

174. Impact of EMU on Selected Non–European Union Countries, by R. Feldman, K. Nashashibi, R. Nord, P. Allum, D. Desruelle, K. Enders, R. Kahn, and H. Temprano-Arroyo. 1998.

173. The Baltic Countries: From Economic Stabilization to EU Accession, by Julian Berengaut, Augusto Lopez-Claros, Françoise Le Gall, Dennis Jones, Richard Stern, Ann-Margret Westin, Effie Psalida, Pietro Garibaldi. 1998.

172. Capital Account Liberalization: Theoretical and Practical Aspects, by a staff team led by Barry Eichengreen and Michael Mussa, with Giovanni Dell'Ariccia, Enrica Detragiache, Gian Maria Milesi-Ferretti, and Andrew Tweedie. 1998.

171. Monetary Policy in Dollarized Economies, by Tomás Baliño, Adam Bennett, and Eduardo Borensztein. 1998.

170. The West African Economic and Monetary Union: Recent Developments and Policy Issues, by a staff team led by Ernesto Hernández-Catá and comprising Christian A. François, Paul Masson, Pascal Bouvier, Patrick Peroz, Dominique Desruelle, and Athanasios Vamvakidis. 1998.

169. Financial Sector Development in Sub-Saharan African Countries, by Hassanali Mehran, Piero Ugolini, Jean Phillipe Briffaux, George Iden, Tonny Lybek, Stephen Swaray, and Peter Hayward. 1998.

168. Exit Strategies: Policy Options for Countries Seeking Greater Exchange Rate Flexibility, by a staff team led by Barry Eichengreen and Paul Masson with Hugh Bredenkamp, Barry Johnston, Javier Hamann, Esteban Jadresic, and Inci Ötker. 1998.

167. Exchange Rate Assessment: Extensions of the Macroeconomic Balance Approach, edited by Peter Isard and Hamid Faruqee. 1998

166. Hedge Funds and Financial Market Dynamics, by a staff team led by Barry Eichengreen and Donald Mathieson with Bankim Chadha, Anne Jansen, Laura Kodres, and Sunil Sharma. 1998.

165. Algeria: Stabilization and Transition to the Market, by Karim Nashashibi, Patricia Alonso-Gamo, Stefania Bazzoni, Alain Féler, Nicole Laframboise, and Sebastian Paris Horvitz. 1998.

164. MULTIMOD Mark III: The Core Dynamic and Steady-State Model, by Douglas Laxton, Peter Isard, Hamid Faruqee, Eswar Prasad, and Bart Turtelboom. 1998.

163. Egypt: Beyond Stabilization, Toward a Dynamic Market Economy, by a staff team led by Howard Handy. 1998.

162. Fiscal Policy Rules, by George Kopits and Steven Symansky. 1998.

161. The Nordic Banking Crises: Pitfalls in Financial Liberalization? by Burkhard Dress and Ceyla Pazarbaşıoğlu. 1998.

160. Fiscal Reform in Low-Income Countries: Experience Under IMF-Supported Programs, by a staff team led by George T. Abed and comprising Liam Ebrill, Sanjeev Gupta, Benedict Clements, Ronald McMorran, Anthony Pellechio, Jerald Schiff, and Marijn Verhoeven. 1998.

159. Hungary: Economic Policies for Sustainable Growth, Carlo Cottarelli, Thomas Krueger, Reza Moghadam, Perry Perone, Edgardo Ruggiero, and Rachel van Elkan. 1998.

158. Transparency in Government Operations, by George Kopits and Jon Craig. 1998.

157. Central Bank Reforms in the Baltics, Russia, and the Other Countries of the Former Soviet Union, by a staff team led by Malcolm Knight and comprising Susana Almuiña, John Dalton, Inci Otker, Ceyla Pazarbaşıoğlu, Arne B. Petersen, Peter Quirk, Nicholas M. Roberts, Gabriel Sensenbrenner, and Jan Willem van der Vossen. 1997.

156. The ESAF at Ten Years: Economic Adjustment and Reform in Low-Income Countries, by the staff of the International Monetary Fund. 1997.

155. Fiscal Policy Issues During the Transition in Russia, by Augusto Lopez-Claros and Sergei V. Alexashenko. 1998.

154. Credibility Without Rules? Monetary Frameworks in the Post–Bretton Woods Era, by Carlo Cottarelli and Curzio Giannini. 1997.

153. Pension Regimes and Saving, by G.A. Mackenzie, Philip Gerson, and Alfredo Cuevas. 1997.

152. Hong Kong, China: Growth, Structural Change, and Economic Stability During the Transition, by John Dodsworth and Dubravko Mihaljek. 1997.

151. Currency Board Arrangements: Issues and Experiences, by a staff team led by Tomás J.T. Baliño and Charles Enoch. 1997.

150. Kuwait: From Reconstruction to Accumulation for Future Generations, by Nigel Andrew Chalk, Mohamed A. El-Erian, Susan J. Fennell, Alexei P. Kireyev, and John F. Wilson. 1997.

149. The Composition of Fiscal Adjustment and Growth: Lessons from Fiscal Reforms in Eight Economies, by G.A. Mackenzie, David W.H. Orsmond, and Philip R. Gerson. 1997.

148. Nigeria: Experience with Structural Adjustment, by Gary Moser, Scott Rogers, and Reinold van Til, with Robin Kibuka and Inutu Lukonga. 1997.

147. Aging Populations and Public Pension Schemes, by Sheetal K. Chand and Albert Jaeger. 1996.

146. Thailand: The Road to Sustained Growth, by Kalpana Kochhar, Louis Dicks-Mireaux, Balazs Horvath, Mauro Mecagni, Erik Offerdal, and Jianping Zhou. 1996.

145. Exchange Rate Movements and Their Impact on Trade and Investment in the APEC Region, by Takatoshi Ito, Peter Isard, Steven Symansky, and Tamim Bayoumi. 1996.

144. National Bank of Poland: The Road to Indirect Instruments, by Piero Ugolini. 1996.

143. Adjustment for Growth: The African Experience, by Michael T. Hadjimichael, Michael Nowak, Robert Sharer, and Amor Tahari. 1996.

142. Quasi-Fiscal Operations of Public Financial Institutions, by G.A. Mackenzie and Peter Stella. 1996.

141. Monetary and Exchange System Reforms in China: An Experiment in Gradualism, by Hassanali Mehran, Marc Quintyn, Tom Nordman, and Bernard Laurens. 1996.

140. Government Reform in New Zealand, by Graham C. Scott. 1996.

139. Reinvigorating Growth in Developing Countries: Lessons from Adjustment Policies in Eight Economies, by David Goldsbrough, Sharmini Coorey, Louis Dicks-Mireaux, Balazs Horvath, Kalpana Kochhar, Mauro Mecagni, Erik Offerdal, and Jianping Zhou. 1996.

138. Aftermath of the CFA Franc Devaluation, by Jean A.P. Clément, with Johannes Mueller, Stéphane Cossé, and Jean Le Dem. 1996.

137. The Lao People's Democratic Republic: Systemic Transformation and Adjustment, edited by Ichiro Otani and Chi Do Pham. 1996.

136. Jordan: Strategy for Adjustment and Growth, edited by Edouard Maciejewski and Ahsan Mansur. 1996.

135. Vietnam: Transition to a Market Economy, by John R. Dodsworth, Erich Spitäller, Michael Braulke, Keon Hyok Lee, Kenneth Miranda, Christian Mulder, Hisanobu Shishido, and Krishna Srinivasan. 1996.

134. India: Economic Reform and Growth, by Ajai Chopra, Charles Collyns, Richard Hemming, and Karen Parker with Woosik Chu and Oliver Fratzscher. 1995.

133. Policy Experiences and Issues in the Baltics, Russia, and Other Countries of the Former Soviet Union, edited by Daniel A. Citrin and Ashok K. Lahiri. 1995.

132. Financial Fragilities in Latin America: The 1980s and 1990s, by Liliana Rojas-Suárez and Steven R. Weisbrod. 1995.

131. Capital Account Convertibility: Review of Experience and Implications for IMF Policies, by staff teams headed by Peter J. Quirk and Owen Evans. 1995.

130. Challenges to the Swedish Welfare State, by Desmond Lachman, Adam Bennett, John H. Green, Robert Hagemann, and Ramana Ramaswamy. 1995.

Note: For information on the title and availability of Occasional Papers not listed, please consult the IMF Publications Catalog or contact IMF Publication Services.